Cure Codependency and Conquer as an Empath

The Ultimate Guide to Codependent Survival and
Empath Empowerment Through Self Healing and
Recovery from Narcissistic Relationships

LEANNE WALTERS

Leanne Walters
Books

TABLE OF CONTENTS

INTRODUCTION

As human beings, we rely a lot on relationships. They are the single greatest social difference between us and every other organism on the planet. The sophisticated relationships that humans hold enable us to synchronize our aims and thoughts much faster than any other species on Mother Earth. This ability alone has enabled us to form complex associations and build large social networks.

Each person exists as the core element within a group or network that contains his friends, family members, and associates. The way we relate with these people in our life determines to a very large extent how much we enjoy or suffer in life. The way we talk, think, eat, act, and react to circumstances are all affected by the relationships we hold with those closest to us. In an ideal situation, the people around us are meant to help us achieve our potentials. They are there to encourage us and support our dreams. They are there to look after us and give us fresh inspiration to strive for our goals.

Conversely, we are also there to help them when they are down. Spouse, friend, colleague, or children, we have a moral obligation to help them out when they are battling any life crisis. We are supposed to be their backbones, and pull them back on their feet when they get knocked to the ground.

However, what happens when you lose yourself in the process of rescuing your loved ones? What happens when you can no longer differentiate between helping the people around you, and getting consumed by their problems to the point where you can no longer separate your needs from theirs? What is our fate when we lose control of the rational process of care, help, and concern, and become slaves to the needs of those around us?

Codependency describes the state of affairs where you lose your own identity in the process of trying to help out a loved one with their problems. A codependent individual is ready to go any length, however dangerous and counterproductive, to feel needed. He burns himself out, in a very negative way, to *help* other people.

As a ten-year-old girl, I came in contact for the first time with a codependent relationship. My father was an alcoholic who came home each night drunk to the bone and drenched in cheap booze. When he first picked up the drinking habit, mother would sit up each night to wait for him to arrive. Each night, from behind curtains, I watched them shout at one another. Mother would sit up after my dad must have passed out or slept, and cry. She would appear heartbroken, and at the end of her tether. Even as a child, it was obvious to me that she couldn't bear that much pain and misery, but she did.

As the months went by though, I noticed a change; Mother grew resigned to her fate. There were no longer any rows when my father came home. In fact, she seemed to be paying more attention to him than usual without complaining. She became a caregiver to him and made his drinking habit her primary duty. She bought him booze to drink at home and stay away from the pub. He adhered for a few days before he went loose again. Yet, Mother never complained again. She had gained some emotional satisfaction from being in charge of him. Her work began to suffer, and her health became poor. She devoted herself totally to the care of my father and gave him a springboard to drink even further. She became codependent, and it took away her life.

Codependency asks way too much out of you; it requires that you subjugate your basic needs to fight what is often a losing battle on behalf of people who do not even want you in the battle. Things are even worse if you are overly empathetic. Empathetic people are dialed into human emotions on a much more sensitive frequency than the average fellow on the streets. They can discern and perceive emotional undercurrents fast, and they get affected easily by what their sensors are picking up. Unfortunately, these sensors seem to be even more sensitive when they are picking up negative feelings. Even without spoken words, an empathetic individual can discern sadness, panic, or anxiety from the people around them. That would not be a problem ordinarily, but empathetic people have a way of multiplying the sensations they pick and making it theirs.

Add codependency and empathy together, and you have a potent mix that will blow away any inner peace you possess. They are traits that must be gotten rid of when they are taken to the extreme. Care and concern are basic character traits for you as a human; they confirm that you care for those around you. However, when they are taken to the extreme, they can become double-edged weapons against you. When you lose sight of the shore while trying to save another from turbulent waters, it is time to head back to shore.

Do you find yourself constantly asking questions like, "Am I codependent?" "How may I help others without becoming too attached?" "How do I stop being an enabler?" "How can I learn to observe the emotions of others without getting consumed in them?" "How can I rebuild my mental psyche and protect it from the dangers of being highly empathetic?"

If you have these questions and more, then I wrote this book with you in mind. My mum was the first codependent individual I knew. In the years after, I have witnessed first-hand the effects of being codependent or too empathetic. I have witnessed the horrors that come with not being able to draw a rational limit for the care and concern you dispense.

At the age of twenty-seven, I took a most-monumental step in rebuilding my mental health; I got divorced! I am famous today as Leanne Walters, an addiction and mental health specialist. However, the three years I spent married do not support the fame my name has brought me. For three years, I supported an addicted spouse who was forever absent except when he was absolutely high. In the beginning, I kept making excuses for him. He was absent because he couldn't avoid it. The pressure at work was getting on his nerves. He's only gone for a few bottles.

Soon though, I couldn't ignore the problem any longer. Instead of being the helping hand he needed to pull him out, I descended into a pit of mental chaos. I wanted him to be clean once again. Yet, I dreaded the day he wouldn't need me any longer. I was torn, and I passively encouraged his addictions. In fact, I did more than that. I was already slightly addicted before I met him but being codependent kicked up my own addictions big time. It brought out the worst in me and changed my life for the worse before my own eyes.

You do not need to go through such a similar phase before tackling your codependency and empathetic tendencies. I know exactly what it feels like to be lost within the life of another. I know how frustrating it is to be emotionally connected to everyone around you at once. I know how hard it is to be a true empath or remain codependent. It is a perfect recipe for unbelievable levels of physical stress, emotional distress, mental knockdowns, and a collapse of all psychological checkpoints.

You no longer have to suffer forever for the actions of the people around you. You are responsible for those around you, but only after you have taken responsibility for your own psychological needs. You need to relearn how to offer care and help without getting consumed in the process. It is the only way out of the dark pit that is codependency.

Approximately thirty years ago, I walked into my first group therapy session, feeling apprehensive about what to expect. I felt unsure, but today I stand as living proof that you can recover from codependency too. Over the last two decades, after I recovered from my addictions and codependency, I have spent my time helping hundreds of other people with the same problems to live a fruitful, hassle-free life once more. The successes I have recovered have helped me to understand the basic psychology at play in codependent people and empaths. It is the expertise I have gained within this period, and my personal experiences that I have compiled to create a shortcut for you out of the mental prison that codependency and empathy can put you in.

When it comes to codependency, things are not helped by the fact that there is a lot of confusion concerning the term. Some say virtually everyone is codependent in one way or the other. Other authorities deem it a full-blown mental illness, while some see it as a mere negative social trait. These confusions have made it harder for the average sufferer to seek treatment. Also, most books on the subject are way too academic to be of much practical use for self-help. I have taken note of this in preparing this guide for you.

This book offers you the best tutelage in how to kick these two destructive habits in less than a month. Your full recovery will probably take a bit more than that to be complete, but this book sets you on the true path to emotional and mental control. With the time-proven techniques that I have helped other people apply to their daily lives, there is no reason why you should not be able to recover and love people within safe limits once again.

However, if you must retake control of your mental processes, then you need to start now. As character traits, codependency and empathy cause progressive damage on an almost daily basis. To get rid of them, you need high levels of discipline and commitment. They will not go away either until you make them. With each passing day, they grow deeper into you and become an even firmer part of your personality. That is why you should not drop this book until you have fully understood what you are up against and committed yourself to the recovery program advocated within the book.

With help from my personalized techniques, experiences, and strategies, you will be on the road to recovery faster than you could have ever imagined. My teachings have yielded outstanding results over the years, and it only made sense for me to put them all into a clear and concise reading for people like yourself who I do not have physical access to. Every chapter in this book will take you one step closer to learning why you are who you are now, and how you can deal with it and regain control and overcome the fear caused by these traits.

I took the long path to recovery. I tried everything from brute force, to self-hypnosis. I went through high and low points while recovering, and followed some of the most outlandish advice ever written, all to no avail. Luckily, I found a path out of the woods. I learned how to be happy once again, and live life to the fullest. I taught myself how to love myself again, and then, how to love the people around me in a way that ensures I am whole at all times. I have spent the better part of my life attending therapy sessions for people in the same shoes I was once in, and teaching them my approach to resounding success.

This book saves you the stress of taking the same long path I took or spending years experimenting with different recovery approaches. It tells you everything you have always wanted to know about toxic relationships and how to get divested from them. I also make a promise here; this book will try to save all the toxic relationships you have. It is only those that are damaged beyond repair that I will teach you to spot and ditch.

What are you waiting for? Turn the pages already and let us get started on your recovery. Your recovery starts from the time you turn the next page.

Good luck!

ARE YOU CODEPENDENT OR AN EMPATH? TWO SIMILAR, BUT VERY DIFFERENT TRAITS

Today, I have twenty years of professional experience in mental health and addiction recovery, but I have been the unlucky victim of quite a few conditions myself. In particular, I went through a rough childhood that left indelible foundations for negative empathy and codependency to develop within me later on in life.

I could give you dictionary definitions for both conditions, but I wouldn't do better than what the world's army of lexicographers has done already. Instead, let me use an example from my own life to differentiate both.

As I detailed in the introduction, I was brought up in an unhealthy family environment – it wasn't like our family was the worst on the block I grew up in, but the atmosphere did leave a large mark on me. My dad picked up a drinking habit that he never got rid of until it eventually killed him when I was around thirteen years old. That was the genesis of the toxic atmosphere.

Initially, my mum tried her best to wean him off. She

cried, cajoled and entreated him. They had furious rows that never yielded anything besides obstinacy and a lot of tears. My dad was not a bad father – I loved (up till now) him for he always took good care of us when he was sober. However, each evening, he would go out and return in the dead of night, soaked to the bone in booze.

After about a year, the frequency of the rows decreased – and no, it was not because his drinking problem subsided. Rather, Mother had changed tact and tried to use the carrot approach. She made accommodations that sought to help him reduce his intake rather than cut it off. Most of her methods never really worked, but one thing changed. No longer was she bitter about his habit. She became more concerned about his safety rather than the habit itself.

She would sit up and take his coat when he arrived. She would fix him a bath if he was not too far gone to want one. I think she thought she could break him by playing his game but by her rules. That not only failed; mother herself became so enmeshed that on nights when he wasn't out drinking, a cloud came over her face. She grew to like the role of caregiver that she had thrust upon herself.

Suddenly, Father's drinking was less important compared to what he chose to do after each drinking spree. She lived to worry over him instead of working on cutting him off as she had initially sought. She became dependent on his dependence on her.

The relationship between my parents was classical codependency. It heated our house and taught me a few things about human nature. Most importantly though, it actually changed me too. As a young girl, I loved the air at home before Father started drinking. After he became addicted to the bottle, everything changed. The rows, accusations, and fights got to me and left me scared. I stood behind the curtains many nights as my parents traded words and threats of violence. I was scared, alone and desolate in turns. Most importantly, I grew a long nose for smelling out trouble. I knew when to disappear from the living room. I knew how to make myself so little that I wasn't noticed during discussions. I cried in bed in the night, sad at events. Yet, each morning, as I grew older, I would be first out of bed to do the household chores. I tried my best to rectify things in my own little way, but it never went noticed. That was the beginning of the heightened sensitivity that was to characterize my adult life. I became so sensitive and tuned to the feelings of those around me that I wouldn't do anything that could upset anyone, even if not doing it did upset me.

The summary of my childhood was that I had an addicted father, a codependent mother and I was to become too sensitive and empathetic as a result of my experiences growing up in an unhealthy atmosphere. As I grew up, these traits never left me. Things weren't helped by the fact that I grew addictions to drugs and a host of other destructive traits early in my teenage years. I grew codependent in almost all subsequent relationships I had after that.

Now, perhaps we can still get in a few dictionary definitions, eh?

———————

As human beings, each of us is different in terms of psychological makeup and emotional characteristics. While there is no single factor that determines our inherent traits, two particular features stand out; our upbringing and the relationships we hold with the people closest to us as we grow up.

If both factors present you with a healthy balance as you grow up, it becomes easier for you to maintain equally healthy relationships as you go on in life. It makes you mentally balanced to be able to draw benefits from the relationships you hold while also contributing a healthy quota in return. It allows you to provide emotional support to peers and family members without draining out and allows you to take back without burning out the source.

Unfortunately, things are not always as smooth as they could be. This can lead to character faults and gaps that make relationships toxic, emotionally-draining affairs rather than the support blocks they are meant to be.

Codependency and empathy fall into this gap of potentially-limiting character traits. Unfortunately, most people cannot differentiate between them, or do not even know they have one of these traits. The first task for me is to delineate both for you clearly.

Codependency is said to exist when an emotionally-parasitic relationship exists between two people; with one being dependent and the other party being the codependent individual. In almost all cases, the dependent partner is often referred to as a narcissist and usually has one serious addiction or the other. The codependent individual, on the other hand, is guilty of one major sin- over-caring for the dependent individual. In the process of helping the dependent individual out of the pit of addiction/negative habits, they begin to derive satisfaction from being the hero of the hour.

They grow so used to this feeling that they begin to crave the chance to help out. In that way, some people refer to codependents as "help and care addicts" who cannot get their fill of pleasure until they feel they have been left in charge or asked to rescue a loved one or friend. The addiction becomes so real and concrete that they begin to plan their life and daily activities around the dependent partner. With time, negative emotions like fear, irritability, total dependence, emotional and nervous breakdowns, and foul moods become the currency of their life as the dependent partner remains unable or unwilling to satisfy their needs.

Spurred on by the initial need to help close ones, codependency becomes a parasitic arrangement; the codependent is no longer truly interested in seeing the dependent or narcissistic partner back to normal. They thrive off the feeling of being needed. They need to be needed to feel satisfied. Therein lies the limitless pitfalls that abound in codependency. These pitfalls were summarized by Knudson and Terrell (2012) when they said, "codependents, busy taking care of others, forget to take care of themselves, resulting in a disturbance of identity development."

On the other hand, empathy is essentially a positive trait when it is not taken to excessive levels. Empathy, at a basic level, refers to the ability to feel another person's pain or emotional discomfort. In that way, we are all supposed to have empathetic tendencies. A perfectly balanced individual should be able to connect with the pains and suffering of other people and use that as a basis for developing true compassion, selflessness and the will to help others out. That is what healthy empathy looks like. However, in the context of this book, and indeed psychology discussions, the classic empath takes the sensory ability beyond safe levels.

How would you like to have a radar that can detect emotional undercurrents in whomever you meet? Sounds great, right? It would seem to be a license to understand people and their sources of discontent better, right?

However, if this radar not only picks up signals but bathes you in them, how easy would it be for you to deal with emotional feedback from all the people you meet, stranger or acquaintance, friend or foe? You must get the picture now. Imagine the emotional baggage of ten people being thrown at you in one jolt. How easy would that be to deal with and sort yourself out?

That is exactly what empaths have to deal with on a daily basis. The human mind may be the most sophisticated, and efficient biological organ ever known, but even our brains have a breaking limit. When you are under the constant deluge of emotional signals that you take to be yours, certain mental safeguards collapse to leave you unduly stressed out. With no filter in place to effectively screen out excess emotional baggage, you may find yourself collapsing under the weight of the expectations you have placed on yourself.

Codependency certainly looks like the most destructive trait at first glance, but that is only half of the story. Empaths have a heightened chance of becoming codependent compared to others without the trait. Since they have an over-sensitized emotional detection system, they take codependency to staggering levels. Easily hurt, and not missing a thing, empaths make for the worst forms of codependents.

However, this is not to say both terms are distinct and interchangeable. The presence of one does not preclude the presence of the other. You can be empathetic without becoming codependent, and while empathy is often the initial stage of codependency, not all codependents are empathetic.

The Origins of Codependency

To better contrast between both traits, let us take a look at their respective origins. I use "Origin" with all caution as no psychological issue ever has one single origin. In most cases, they are often the end product of a number of interplaying factors. Let us look at the most important factors in both cases.

With codependency, the greatest risk factor is in childhood development and family characteristics. Research has found out that the vast majority of codependent individuals grew up in dysfunctional family settings where they were robbed of the pure freedom that comes with childhood. Children born in families with repressive rules and injunctions are at risk of being stifled. It is even worse when one or both parents are addicts or battle mental illness.

In such scenarios, children are made to grow mentally too rapidly. That means they skip many developmental steps in the process and become emotionally-deficient as they grow older. Such children may be forced to become caregivers too early in life. A drunkard as a father, a drug addict as a mother, these sorts of situations can thrust children into caregiving roles too fast for their own good.

Alternatively, even in the absence of addictions, families that hold children to certain *ideal* standards, or set them impossible aims can cause severe, chronic damage to the psyche of such children. When the family setting becomes suffused with so many negative restrictions, kids turn inwards on a destructive streak that eats away their self-esteem faster than anything else can at that stage of life. What does that tell you?

They may have to become used to being people-pleasers very early in life. They try to conform, and that changes their normal constitution. Very early in life, they get taught to put others before themselves. They are shown why they must consider the family interests before theirs, even when the interests are not entirely right.

When children are exposed to such conditions, they learn to view relationships as an avenue to subdue themselves to the needs of the people around them. Therefore, if in the future they are unfortunate enough to come in contact with narcissists, they have a lower resistance threshold and capitulate easily. For them, it is a continuation of what they started as a young child. Other factors may contribute to the development of codependency, but this is the most important denominator.

The Origins of Empathy

Empathy is present in almost everyone in small traces. It is the reason we can all live in a society with regards to one another's rights and duties. However, some are born with naturally-sharpened senses that can detect sub-currents faster than even the brain can comprehend the signals. Unfortunately, empaths not only detect, but they also imbibe and get engulfed in the negative signals they pick up.

How do people become that sensitive? In the two decades I have spent helping people back onto their feet, I have found three main ways empaths become so sensitive.

1.   Inherent nature

There is such a thing as a natural empath. These people are born with that extra-sensitive gene. From birth, it is possible for an infant to show extra sensitivity to stimuli such as light, crowded spaces, and cluttered environments. Such sensitive babies may grow to show the empathetic tendency within them typically. They need very little prompting to develop the negative side of their unique personality. We are all born with our own unique personality traits; if yours include extra sensitivity, then the chances are that your empathy is never too far below the surface.

2.   Genetics

Empathy as a trait, can be handed down from parents to offspring. Whether this is as a result of genetic material transfer, or simply induction from living with and observing parents since childhood, children of empathetic people are just as likely to develop such traits.

Now, the two points above are further potentiated if the parents are supportive and help their wards nurture a spirit of genuine care and compassion.

3. Trauma

Blunt trauma and stressful events during childhood can also cause an increase in sensitivity levels as an adult. Getting exposed to abuse, emotional, physical, or sexual, can break the healthy defense system that we are all born with. Being on the receiving end of unsatisfied hunger for genuine care and concern can twist things around and wear down a child. Being naturally sensitive as children, humans are likely to take note of this and develop a sixth sense for determining the emotional state of the people they meet. This will serve as a defense mechanism that can help to preempt initial hostility and sound the alarm to vanish out of sight. Importantly, this can grow into adulthood with the child and make him/her extra-sensitive and more prone to emotional injury and pain.

It does not take rocket science to spot that my empathy grew out of the third way. I grew so attuned to the emotions of my parents that I could walk into a room and sense right away that a verbal row had just gone down a few moments before I came in.

At that point, I couldn't describe the intuitive ability to

sense things out of people's minds, but I knew it was an unusual talent. It was not until many years after that, I learned the proper terms, "empathy" and "codependency" used to describe the state of affairs I was in as a child.

To round up the chapter, codependence and empathy can activate each-other, each can exist alone solely without the other, and both can occur at the same time in a single individual to marked destructive potentials if not promptly managed. However, they are two distinct conditions despite the obvious similarities.

UNDERSTANDING WHAT TRUE CODEPENDENCY LOOKS AND FEELS LIKE

I was thirteen and in high school when my dad died of liver disease brought on by alcoholism. Regardless of his faults, he had been a great father to me and I took his loss to heart in a big way. After his death, I couldn't handle the stress. At school, I felt lonely and unaccepted by the kids there. Whenever I went to school, I felt like I did not belong with the other kids and they did not seem to like me. Deep within me, I harbored the secret desire of wanting to please those kids, gain their approval, and be like them.

It was at the heart of all this that Lucy came to me. She was one of the kids I had been admiring then, so you can imagine my happiness when she approached me for friendship. I couldn't even contemplate saying "no" to her. Soon, Lucy introduced me to the world of alcohol and drugs. Initially, I resisted, but after the first puff, I was hooked for good.

Despite the fact that I knew the effects alcohol and

drugs have on a person's health after my father's experience, I could not bring myself to say "No" to Lucy. I worked hard to gain her approval and put a smile on her face as we drank and did drugs. Having a true *friend* and her attention was more important to me than whatever effect that lifestyle could have on me. All I wanted then was to be with her because there was always one new drug to test out or the other.

I did not even want to picture an end to our friendship. I was always at her beck and call, and eager to do as she said. I felt like she was the only person in the world who cared for me and I would not be able to survive without her attention. I could see my life falling apart, breaking into tiny pieces before my own very eyes, but I did not care. Such is the helplessness of codependents.

It took an almost fatal episode of overdosage to wake me up. It was that episode that finally jarred me to my senses. That was when I realized that not only did I have to fix my addiction problems, I also had to deal with my codependency, which was the root of my addiction. It was until I looked for help that I came to know that my relationship with Lucy was not even genuine friendship, but codependency.

Like many other abnormal traits and conditions, most codependent people do not know that they are even codependent. They see nothing wrong or abnormal with the way they behave or the kind of relationships they have. They assume that their behavior is okay, or that they deserve the kind of treatment they get in their relationships. A lot of times, codependents are either unwilling or seemingly unable to review the toxic relationships they hold for the better.

In this chapter, I will explain to you what it feels like to be codependent. I will explain in detail the kind of behavior that codependents exhibit and how you can be certain of your codependency status.

Before then, let's delve once again into the nitty-gritty of the principles underlying codependency.

The first thing to note is that if you are in a relationship with an addict of either alcohol, drugs, sex or gambling; or if you have a family member who is addicted to the aforementioned things or chronically sick, then you have a higher chance of becoming codependent. I don't mean to say that all people that are in such situations are codependent. However, being in such kinds of relationships gives you a much higher chance of becoming codependent than individuals who are not in such relationships.

Codependency makes you live your life for one sole purpose, and that is to get the approval of that one person whom you have made the center of your existence. That person could be your partner, spouse, parent, sibling or even a friend. In such kind of relationships, all you want to do is to please them, even at the expense of your own happiness or well-being. You go out of your way to make sure that they are happy with you. You lose your identity and neglect your own needs and wants. You feel like you cannot live without them, or that you need them and their presence in your life in order for you to survive. There is nothing that gives you satisfaction other than them; nothing that is not related to them makes you feel whole. It is like you have a mantra that says, "my needs don't matter, let them be happy."

Let me correct one wrong notion. There are two broad schools of thought when it comes to the actual contribution that affected people make to their codependence. The first line of thought categorizes all codependent people as willing/weak contributors to their own plight. The second line of thought suggests that codependents are victims of improper upbringing and a narcissistic partner. Both conclusions have their own merits and strong points. However, the main point to note is that codependency is not essentially a terrible or bad trait.

It is, in fact, concern taken too far. It is an indictment on the grounds of over-caring. This is not to absolve codependent individuals of all the blame. However, codependency arises from the innate desire to reach out and support those we care for. Unfortunately, if these people are narcissists or addicts, there is a chance that they will drain more than the share of care you are willing to give. There is a high probability that they will take all you are willing to give and then ask for more commitment and support beyond your limits.

Unfortunately for codependent people, a weak upbringing endows them with weak and porous borders that cannot stand up to the rigors of what is being demanded of them. So, they cave inwards but strive to remain unfazed and strong on the outside. The codependents in society are often wrongly labeled as strong. For instance, a wife supporting a husband with a chronic drug addiction may be labeled "strong". Such misplaced praise endows codependents with further reason and drive to burn themselves up to light the way for others who are not even interested in taking the path.

In addition, all human beings have twenty-three pairs of chromosomes responsible for coding our genetic matter. By way of analogy, I like to suggest that codependents have an extra chromosome – the hero chromosome – which infects them with a desire to play the hero at all times. They feel they are responsible for everyone around them – the drunk spouse, the friend who cannot seem to hold a relationship for two weeks, the lazy colleague at work, or the ill sibling. They turn themselves to candles, burning out to light the way for others to thrive. They go to extra lengths to render help and care to the utter detriment of their personal wellbeing. They do this without expecting appreciation *per se* – they just want to be needed the next time as well. Spurred on by the hero chromosome, a true codependent can go to just about any length to rescue even people they are not very close to.

Ten traits of codependent people

Let us look at some common characteristics of codependent people. If you find any of the following traits within you, or they hold true in your relationships, then it is an indication that you may already be on the way to codependency if you are not there already.

1) **Low self-esteem**

Do you always feel that you are inferior and that other people are so much better than you? Do you feel like you are not good enough and your partner is better than you? Does that feeling of insecurity make you stay in relationships irrespective of the state of the relationship? Low esteem is a vital indicator of codependency. It can make you feel insecure and ashamed of who you are even when you have not done anything wrong. If you feel like your partner is doing you a great favor by being in a relationship with someone as miserable as you think you are, then you have to start planning how to become self-reliant, because clearly you already have the seeds of codependency sown within you. The typical codependent individual seeks to subjugate his own

34

rights and needs to other people's because he lacks the esteem needed to make a stand when necessary.

2) **People-pleaser**

It is a good thing to want to please people and earn their love – it is something we all do. However, when you seem always to want to please others at your own detriment, then there has to be a further inquiry. If you find it absolutely impossible to say "no" to other people, then you may already be walking a thin line. Do you understand when you have to pull out and let others take care of their problems? Typical codependents are unable to do this– not being able to hold back from helping others is a clear sign of codependency. You tend even to forget your own needs and wants in order to please others. The only thing you seem to know how to do in a relationship is give, without ever receiving anything in return.

3) **Weak Boundaries**

One of the problems codependents face is finding it difficult to set boundaries or draw lines they are not willing to allow other people to cross. If you are codependent, you will find it difficult to set personal boundaries in your life or relationships. You may be scared of setting limits because you are afraid that it may cost you the relationships you do not want to lose. As such, you become tolerant of abuse and maltreatment because you are afraid of what marking your own boundaries will do to your relationships.

4) Over-The-Top Reactions

As a codependent, you will tend to react to things more than other people do. You think that you understand what everyone goes through and how much you need to help them out of it. You tend to feel like you have an obligation to react to people's feeling and emotions. You become an emotional wet sponge absorbing everything thrown at it. You tend to feel people's hurt even more than they themselves do because you already believe you are responsible for their emotional well-being. As humans, it is natural to feel sympathetic towards someone in distress, but for a codependent, it is a whole sense of responsibility to alleviate other people's problems.

5) Obsession

Obsession can be a sign of codependency. If you are codependent, you may find yourself obsessed with your partner or a particular family member. You never seem to be able to get them out of your mind. You are always obsessed with new methods to please them, or making up for past events. They are just the center of your existence. In one way or the other, everything you do is related to pleasing them. Even a slight change in their mood can determine the outcome of your entire day. You tend to keep track of their lives and give them advice, even when your advice never gets used or appreciated. In short, everything around you is automatically wired to them.

6) Dependency

Codependents always feel the need to be loved or supported by someone. They can hardly stand the thought of being alone or without a particular person in their life. They depend on other people's love or presence to feel whole. They rely on others to make decisions about their lives, to be happy, to feel free. In fact, it is almost as if they rely on others to simply survive. If you feel any of these, then you are on the codependent train.

7) Emotional Distress

Being codependent can make you experience a lot of negative emotions. The fear of losing the love or attention of the person you love may make you become anxious. Your inability to please or appease them can make you feel sad or even depressed. You may be anxious because you are afraid that you will not be loved or wanted, or that the person you so much need in your life is going to leave you. All these combine to leave you largely unstable and emotionally distressed most of the time.

8) Overindulgence

If you are codependent, you will tend to let your partner get away with all the horrible things they do. You never seem to get the courage to tell them when they are wrong or point out to them the bad decisions they are making, even if it affects you. Instead, you take up the responsibility of cleaning up their mess and covering it up for them. The greater the mess, the more irritated and responsible you feel for it.

9) An addictive partner

Being in a relationship or married to a partner who has some form of addiction is a classic requirement for codependency to be established. If you are in a relationship with an addicted person and somehow, you feel responsible for their addictions, codependency may have set in. Such relationships may be harmful to you, yet you cannot seem to let go of them despite the knock-on effects. In most cases, you may not even notice the effects that such relationships have on you. It is okay to accept people for who they are, but when who they are is toxic for you, that's not being considerate. It is being codependent.

10) Overbearing Control Freaks

The job remit for a codependent is total concern and care. So, a typical codependent may feel the need to control what goes on in the partner's life. He wants always to be there to control the current sequence of events. He has this fear that left alone; something terrible may happen to his dependents. Or at best, he feels his dependent partner cannot control the situation alone.

He wants to be at the forefront each time rescuing the people around him. Most times, he rationalizes his codependence with the excuse that the partner needs him to survive all their daily struggle. All these combine to make most codependents control-freaks who want to be in the thick of the action each time, every time.

The Acid Test for Your Relationships

If you want to truly discern if you are in a codependent relationship, ask yourself the following questions:

1. Does your satisfaction and sense of purpose stem from making extreme sacrifices to satisfy your partner's needs?

2. Is your partner addicted to drugs or alcohol?

3. Do you struggle with saying "no" to your partner's demands even when you should?

4. Do you cover up your partner's crimes or illegal dealings with drugs or alcohol?

5. Do you feel suffocated or caged in your relationship?

6. Do you turn a deaf ear to some things in your relationships just to avoid arguments?

7. Have you been a victim of directed abuse from your partner in the recent past?

8. Do you get regular anger outbursts even when there is no cue?

9. Do you go with the advice of other people against your own intuition and instinct?

10. Do you find it impossible to decline offers for you to help other people?

11. Do you suffer unexplained anxiety, stress, or depression?

12. Do you find it disconcerting to accept compliments, especially in public?

13. Do you get frustrated and angry when your partner chooses the counsel or company of other people over yours?

Pick a piece of paper and record your answers. If more than five are in the affirmative, you are in a codependent relationship. If it is greater than seven elicited positive answers, then you need to act fast to curb your codependency as it is at alarming levels.

Codependency is no healthy state for a relationship; you need to stamp it out or else stamp the relationship itself out of your life.

THE CORE ELEMENTS AND ABILITIES THAT CONTRIUTE TO BEING AN EMPATH

Let us use an analogy to start this chapter. Imagine that you just took hold of a new television; one that allows you to watch every single channel on the planet irrespective of whether you have made a subscription or not. Great appliance, right? There is only one *slight* problem, though. The television records the images from all the channels on one screen. You do not have the chance to select a particular channel. There is no provision for switching between channels. You must follow all the jumbled-up show at once. How would that feel? Is the television still looking like a worthwhile device after all?

Well, spare a thought for empaths, for the mind of an empath is no different. Tuned into all the visual and sub-visual cues being dropped by everyone they come across with, an empath has problems sorting out all these different emotions at once. That is the source of the cons that come with empathy.

Usually, empathy is no negative trait. Rather it is a positive trait that is supposed to help us feel closer to the people we meet and use that as a launchpad to offer compassion and affection. Unfortunately, for a typical empath, this ability becomes debilitating because he is unable to separate himself from the feelings of other people that he comes in contact with. For instance, an empath may be happy and comfortable this moment and become extremely distressed and sad the next moment because a sad person walked into the room. This extremely sensitive ability to discern and take on the emotions of other people means an empath is highly unlikely to be stable emotionally. They live the emotions of a dozen people in a single mind and body, causing an overload in their mental circuitry.

Every emotion that we put forward as individuals presents its own unique energy and vibrates at a certain frequency. It is why certain emotions can present as an almost tangible aura around us. When we feel sad, for instance, even the air around us can feel particularly heavy. A happy individual could also be thoroughly excited and present a tangible aura of light-headed satisfaction and excitement. It is why one person's spirits can lift the other, even in the absence of genuine empathy. With empaths, therefore, there is an oversensitive tuning fork designed to trap all clues on every frequency around. Therefore, an empath is forever trapped on simultaneous frequencies picking up feelings that are not his and turning them into his own.

Sensitive, willing, and unable to control the data overload, an empath is therefore at genuine risk of a collapse of mental safeguards.

Often, there is confusion between being a genuine empath or a highly-sensitive person (HSP). However similar, the two conditions are not the same. Highly-sensitive people are also attuned to emotions and even physical cues; however, empathy is just one arm (out of four) of being highly sensitive. Therefore, almost all empaths are highly sensitive, while not all HSPs are empaths. Think of it this way; both groups of people are highly sensitive to external emotional stimuli, but an HSP merely receives and does not process them to become his own while empaths process the emotions into their own personal feelings. HSPs receive the cues and do not act on them; they just have a very active antenna. Empaths, on the other hand, download the same signals and then proceed to wallow in them.

The stages of an empathetic response

At the risk of oversimplification, there are three stages to each show of empathy. These are the input, conversion, and empathetic response stages.

• The Input stage

This is the defining stage for empaths, where they pick up cues. In this stage, empaths engage a sixth sense subconsciously which continuously scans for emotions, feelings, and physical pain and brings the attention of the empath to them. The sensation could be positive such as happiness, smiles, or positivity. It could also be deeply negative emotions such as panic, grief, and sadness.

- **The conversion stage**

The average individual who is not empathetic also picks up most of these cues, though on a less-refined scale. However, the difference is that the average individual picks up the cues, examines them, and then dismisses them. They do not get affected beyond a certain limit. Things couldn't be more different with empaths. For empathy to kick in, the mind picks up these cues and translates them into images that cause the empath to want to act or feel the same way. Physiologically, there is a mirror neuron system in the nervous system responsible for the mirroring of the emotions of the people empaths meet. This system causes you to automatically imitate the sensations and cues you are picking up. The system automatically primes you to respond to each sensation in a similar vision. It is the genesis of the entire scope of empathy.

- **The empathetic response stage**

This is the last stage where the manifestations of being an empath show up. In this stage, you get to replicate the sensations you have discerned in the people around you. The reaction can be active where you reach out to try to maintain positive sensations in others or try to correct/fix negative emotions. Most empaths, however, experience a passive response stage. They simply download the sensations they are picking up and make them into their own. They may not make any move to try to fix the source of the negative sensations they are picking up. Instead, they just dissolve in it.

In the context of codependency, though, empathy is a bit different. It is not just passive or active; it is dominating. A codependent empath is one of the worst persons to be psychologically. As a codependent, such an individual is hitched to the needs of a narcissist. When you add the hurt and emotional distress that comes with that to the innate problems of being too sensitive, then there is a mega ton of trouble headed that way. It means nothing escapes your attention, and yet, you do not get any succor or positive feeling from your relationship. Instead, the distress is magnified and counts twice as heavy.

Ten classic traits of empaths

How can you know for certain if you are an empath? Luckily, most empaths are aware that they are very sensitive to emotional feelings from childhood. It is very rare to develop empathetic tendencies in adulthood. Rather, as I have explained in the last chapter, it is often triggered by a latent series of emotional trauma or exists as an inherited trait. In either case, there is a bevy of associated traits that come with the empath package. Let us look at ten of the most common traits that most empaths have.

• Great intuition

Empaths often possess more than the rudimentary five senses that the normal human possesses. Most times, the extra sense is intuition or intuitive at least. Empaths are the most intuitive group of people on the planet. As an empath, you are able to sense when things are happening. By merely shaking hands or even observing another person's face, you can discern far more than the person realizes. As such, an empath may even detect some affection or growing attachment between two other individuals before even the individuals realize that something of the sort is going on. Let me stretch the boundaries a bit further. Empaths are the best at guessing the current state of affairs in a relationship. A cheating partner may get surprised by the sheer intuitiveness of an empath as they are able to discern when the partner's attention towards them has been divided. Long before actual emotional distance sets in to precede a possible separation, an empath may have more than just an inkling of impending storms. Unfortunately, intuition may not always be a positive trait as it does not always come with great news. In fact, it can pile on more of the stress even before the next active stressor is present. As a codependent partner, it can teach you when your attention is not appreciated and cause you further headache, and result in a lowered threshold for emotional injury.

- **The ability to sense the mood in a room**

I have already mentioned this in passing but let me revisit my childhood experience once again. As a child, I grew the superpower of intuition. One of its most practical uses was assessing the emotional undercurrents of every new place I walked into. I could walk into the living room five minutes after a furious row with no visible signs of the row; yet, somewhere within me, I would know things were out of place. Merely conversing with my mum would leave alarm bells ringing in my head. There was no way I could ever shut this power off. I could always tell when there was heavy tension between my parents. My only brother joined a gang and started doing drugs about two years before my dad passed away. By the same intuitive ability, I could tell when he had been out with his *friends*. It didn't matter how vehemently he denied to my mum, or whether they believed him, I only needed to look at him or walk into him to know. There was always this tangible negative feeling I could tap from him that nobody else seemed able to notice. Each time he walked in; I could almost tell with certainty if he had been out doing something he shouldn't be doing. I wondered how my mum never seemed to know for sure. Unfortunately, though, since I was desirous of a happy home, being able to know when there had been a fight, even in my absence, weighed me down considerably and deepened my already-sensitive nose for emotions.

- **Act as walking lie-detectors**

Welcome to a world where you are able to tell when other people are lying to you, or at the very least know that they are economical with the truth. Ideally, that looks like an edge for you, because you can tell when someone is not being truthful. In practical application though, ignorance can be bliss, albeit temporarily. When you have a narcissistic partner that constantly lies or tries to cheat on your intellect, it can be a burden to be able to tell that you are being taken for a yarn once again. Worse, you become better at discerning an individual's lies, the longer you stay with them. So, the chances are that if you are shackled up with a chronic liar, you will spend a lot of time in anguish over their lies. We all love to romanticize our partners as being loyal and honest with us. Having the tool to know that they are not really honest can weigh even the most resilient of people down.

- **Get absorbed and overwhelmed by other people's emotions**

As I explained above, empaths are not the only people capable of discerning undercurrents; all HSPs do that virtually well. In fact, it is why they are called 'sensitive' in the first place. What makes empathy stand out as a potentially-debilitating trait is that empaths don't just understand these emotions, they get co-opted into adopting them as their own. So, each time their partner, friend, or work colleagues, are having a negative feeling and they are close, empaths begin to have the same feeling. It is not just feelings either. An empath can feel physical pain as well. Have you ever walked up to a child crying and almost felt like crying yourself? Even pain or cues picked up from a digital screen such as the net can provoke a strong, corresponding reaction in an empath hundreds of miles away. Things are, therefore worse when a codependent who is already hitched to the needs and wants of a narcissistic partner is also an empath. The combination means that the emotional distress is doubled. Therefore, it is not uncommon to find empaths deeply immersed in other people's troubles, and in the process of finding solutions to these problems. An empath may neglect his own emotional needs to find a fix for a partner's own needs. They get lost in battles that are not theirs when they are codependent, and empathy makes codependency a harder affliction to fight off successfully.

- **Extremely sensitive to negative feedback**

If you are a true codependent, you must know by now that you are highly sensitive and attuned to feedback from people. You want to know what they think of you and your efforts. Well, empathy brings that home and in one large, rude swoop too. With empathy, choosing to receive feedback or not is not even your choice; you get it dumped in your lap whether you want it or not.

Imagine the amount of negative feedback you will pick up as an empath when you work in a toxic environment or live in an unhealthy relationship. That in itself would not have been a problem except for the fact that empaths are naturally sensitive to criticism and negative feedback. So, it becomes imperative that you avoid negative feedback as much as possible since your ability to deal with it is impaired or at best, flawed. Even subtle hints of disdain or disaffection such as smirks or raised eyebrows do not escape you; body language cues also get picked up to contribute to a destabilized mental environment. As an empath, you get the full message of negative feedback even when the subject administering such is not willing to communicate that openly.

- **Empaths are often introverts**

Research has shown that up to 80% of all empaths are introverts. It makes sense when you look at it from a certain angle. If you are so tuned in to every frequency you pass, might it not make more sense for you to limit contact with people, especially in crowded settings. In what we might look upon as an evolutionary measure, most empaths abhor crowded environments and would rather enjoy their own company. This may be because they genuinely enjoy the solitude that comes to them from not engaging many people at once. Empaths are also deep thinkers and creative geniuses; both classes of people have been shown to enjoy solitude as a rule rather than the boisterous, loud atmosphere that comes with venturing out. Even if introversion does not reduce their ability to slip beyond the feeble mental defenses that most people erect, it at least helps you as an empath to limit contact with other people. That is not a very efficient way of resolving the issues that come with empathy, but it is hard to argue against its practical, efficient results.

- **Easy targets for narcissists and manipulators**

Narcissists and manipulators are the worst set of people to surround yourself with, empathy or not. They are often focused on leeching and perching on you to satisfy their own needs and emotional desires. I will discuss them better in the next chapter, but narcissists, as a rule, are drawn towards individuals with weak boundaries. Empaths have very poorly-defined boundaries; so they represent primary targets for emotional manipulators and narcissists. Narcissists can feed off the sensitivity of empaths and use that as a basis and control structure for manipulation and secondary emotional blackmail. Surrounded by narcissists and unable to divest themselves from the negativity that entails, empaths may continue to wither in the presence of such partners. Unfortunately, it is hard to see an empath without narcissists milling about to exploit our heightened capacity for sensitivity.

- **Empaths have problems dishing out rejections and corrections**

This is a no-brainer actually. Since they are sensitive to negative emotions, it is normal to imagine that empaths will try their best to ensure that they are not the source of further emotional distress to other people. For this reason, empaths are often hesitant to dish out justified corrections and rejections. Keenly aware of the fact that they will probably have to share in the emotions that such corrections may generate, empaths may look to avoid confrontative situations. As such, they are unlikely to be found causing rows that can be avoided or creating highly emotional situations that involve them throwing some negative energy or emotions at other people.

- **Stress magnet**

Given the points above, it is pretty obvious that empaths will have to undergo a lot of stress to keep up with their pattern of thoughts. Shackled in a codependent relationship, empaths will find their personal boundaries invaded on a pretty regular basis. Having to care for a narcissist while being extremely sensitive is pretty harrowing. You are able to see through most of their schemes or at least, tell when the schemes are underfoot. To see your efforts at reforming them go unrequited, with commitment on the part of your partner, can also contribute severe psychological stress for you. Physically, the stress of having to look after many people's needs can also drain mental and physical strength pretty quick. Personally, growing up, I avoided parties and social functions for good. I couldn't even last fifteen minutes at social functions before I felt completely drained and empty. As an empath, the sources of physical and psychological stress are too numerous and real to be neglected.

- **Lovers of nature**

This is one trait that has never been fully explained. The general population of empaths seems to cherish nature and natural things. Being in peaceful harmony in a natural environment is pretty soothing compared to the bedlam that is crowds or a narcissistic partner. Most empaths are animal-lovers and would choose to spend time with nature and its structures such as waterfalls, and forests compared to the hustle and bustle of city life. Sadly, this is not always possible.

To round up the chapter, take the following summary. Empathy is a natural feeling that lights up the road to compassion, benevolence, inclusiveness, and sacrifice. However, in empaths, this is taken way beyond healthy borders to represent a genuine threat to the peace and comfort of the empaths themselves.

NARCISSISM AND ABUSE: HOW THEY COULD – AND PROBABLY DO – RELATE TO YOU

Narcissism is, quite frankly, a disorder of the mind. In psychology, it is called the narcissistic personality disorder (a member of a big family of personality disorders); a psychological and mental disorder in which individuals possess an inflated sense of self-importance, an excessive craving for attention and admiration, ill-handled relationships, and a typical lack of empathetic capabilities.

People suffering from the narcissistic personality disorder are often found to exhibit a tremendous amount of confidence; however, behind the façade of self-confidence that they put out lies low self-esteem, which is affected or shaken by the slightest of criticism. Individuals suffering from this disorder (called narcissists) usually encounter problems in many regions of their lives, including their job, relationships, studies, and financial affairs. In addition to these, narcissists are likely to be generally unhappy for large periods of their lives and are usually morose or depressed when they are not shown the kind of admiration they want nor treated to the sort of special favors they think they deserve. Hence, they tend to find their relationships falling short on demands and generally unfulfilling, which forces them to give off negative energy that makes them unpleasant to be with.

Individuals with narcissistic personality disorder differ in terms of their signs and symptoms, as well as the severity of the disorder. However, there are certain signs and symptoms that they all have in common. Some of the most common ones are listed below.

- Perhaps the symptom that eats deepest into the minds of narcissists is their inflated sense of self-importance. They feel and believe that they are superior to other people and should, therefore, be treated as such.

- They have a belief that they are entitled, and have developed, over time, an excessive need to be admired.

- Even without achieving anything, narcissists believe they should be held high and treated as superior to others.

- They tend to exaggerate their achievements and accomplishments.

- They spend large amounts of time occupied with 'dreams' about power, perfection, or success.

- Because of their deep-seated belief that they are superior and special, they tend only to want to associate themselves with people they see as equally special.

- They try to dominate their conversations with other people and look down on the opinions of people they consider inferior to themselves.

- They expect others to acquiesce to their demands without question.

- They use others to get what they want by manipulating and deceiving them.

- They are aloof to the feelings and needs of other people.

- They are usually jealous of others' achievements and at the same time, believe that others are jealous of them.

- Narcissists are typically arrogant or haughty.

- They always want to get a better thing than what others have, for instance, having the best car in the neighborhood.

How Narcissists Attract Codependent and Empathetic Partners

One of the traits of narcissists is their ability to attract people who they can dominate and control – typically empathetic and codependent people. They like to attract these kinds of people because only they can acquiesce to the narcissist's demands without regard to their own. The steps given below show how narcissists attract and keep empaths and codependent people.

1. An empath becomes attracted to a narcissist, and the relationship is kick-started. It is characteristic of empaths to love truly and deeply, and so, in their natural fashion, the empath develops a deep love for the narcissist. The empath feels emotionally stable and fulfilled, having begun the relationship of their dreams and being around the narcissist.

2. The empath begins to feel that they have met the love of their life and thus develops a false notion that their love is reciprocated by the narcissist. They even feel lucky, having found love that 'some people are not so lucky to have.' The narcissist aids in the development of this false notion by creating a façade that makes the empath think that their relationship is something special. Hence, the empath feels so attached that they can't imagine breaking free from the narcissist.

3. The narcissist sometimes creates an illusion that they want this relationship as much as the empath wants it, but this is false, of course. All the narcissist wants is someone who would put in their time, energy, and

passion into a relationship and whom they would be in total control of. This is characteristic of narcissists; they simply want someone to take advantage of.

4. As time goes on, the narcissist, through carefully crafted plans and indirect attacks on the empath, makes the empath continuously feel unconfident in their own abilities, weak, and unable to do even the simplest of things for themselves. The narcissist, in their natural fashion, might never launch a direct attack on the empath; instead, they resort to using indirect attacks through statements such as "I would never want to hurt you, but..." to point out certain mistakes or shortcomings of the empath. In addition, the narcissist would like to control everything that symbolizes power, such as taking care of the bills and making key decisions about purchases. The narcissist would look down on anything the empath feels strongly about, including their interests and the things that form their identity. As time goes on, the empath gradually begins to feel incapable of handling their own life and feels the need to always have the narcissist around. This is when they develop the notion that they are not wanted by any other person.

5. The empath puts everything into the relationship because they feel it is all that

matters. They want to do everything to help and soothe the narcissist, to cheer them up and do everything that pleases them. Because the narcissist has portrayed themselves as a victim of their past relationships, the empath tries their best to make up for all of the narcissist's past woes.

6. The empath possesses a true, loving heart, and wants to help the narcissist as much as they can.

7. From here, it's clear that the relationship is completely focused on the narcissist. The empath begins to realize this too, and slowly but surely, they lose their voice in the relationship. They are afraid to fight for their needs or even talk about them. They place more emphasis on pleasing the narcissist than they do on voicing out their true needs.

8. As they continue to show the narcissist love and attention, the more powerful and in control the narcissist becomes. By now the narcissist has the empath completely in their grasp and the empath dances to the narcissist's tune. What's worse is the empath is unable to detect any problem in the relationship. Hence, they continue to appease the narcissist and fulfill their every need. Codependency is established!

9. Everything goes well until the empath reaches their breaking point. This is when the problem begins. The empath raises their voice for the first time as they can no longer cope in the relationship. They are left distraught as their emotional needs are unfulfilled. The narcissist points out that the empath is being selfish by asking for their own emotional needs to be met, and gets angry.

10. A typical characteristic of narcissists is that they are attention seekers whose needs can never be totally fulfilled. They never seem to get satisfaction in the relationship. Despite that they might get everything they have ever dreamed of – travel around the globe, find the perfect partner, open a lucrative business, or accomplish all of their goals – the narcissist may never get true satisfaction – and they are usually unaware of this fact.

11. When the empath begins to voice out their dissatisfaction with the relationship and demand for more from the narcissist, the narcissist launches a full-blown attack on the empath by calling them demeaning names, such as "crazy" and "dramatic." This sort of behavior is known as gaslighting, and the narcissist uses it to brutal effect.

12. The empath becomes confused as a result of the gaslighting attacks from the narcissist.

They begin to question their own sanity and behavior and even blame themselves for demanding more from the relationship.

13. The empath finds it difficult – if not impossible – to realize that they are being manipulated. They feel that the narcissist is right in all of their judgments.

14. The empath tries to engage in sincere discussions with the narcissist, and every time, the narcissist will try to justify their own stand.

15. After some time, the empath begins to garner strength. They start to evaluate themselves to find out where and how they lost all of the control in their relationship and why they feel so lost. This is the beginning of the empath's transformation.

16. The empath realizes that they are natural healers; they help people heal emotionally through their capacity to know exactly how others are feeling. Sometimes they take their healing ability as a duty and are usually stuck at trying to soothe others.

17. The empath soon comes to understand that their love, care, and affection are not for everyone. They come to know that not everyone who looks to be in need of emotional support truly deserves it, that some people are simply being deceitful and

are not revealing their true selves. Some people go into relationships to put others through difficulties and control them.

18. The empath must now come to terms with the fact that they are in a troubled relationship and a very difficult situation. This is similar to the kinds of situations the narcissist said they were in in their past relationships, but unlike the narcissist, the empath must try to heal and improve.

19. This is most certainly a painful turn of events for the empath as this means they have to start from scratch and work their way up to finding the perfect relationship. But they have the resource of experience and should use it to their advantage.

20. The narcissist goes on with their lives as though nothing has happened, and might even claim total innocence. They soon forget that they were loved truly and deeply by someone. They forget the bond that once existed between themselves and their ex-partner and soon move on to find that with someone else.

21. The narcissist moves on and begins to search for their next victim.

22. On the flip side, the empath should get emotionally and mentally stronger, wiser,

and more careful of who they share their love and time with henceforth.

Note, the scenario above paints a scenario where the empath/codependent is able to successfully survive and outlast a narcissist. Most times, such relationships remain stuck at step 8.

Identifying a Potential Narcissist

At the end of a troubled relationship, the empath is forced to come to terms with the harsh reality that they have wasted their time, effort, and affection. The empath would go on to have a very difficult number of days, weeks, months, even years trying to heal from the wounds inflicted on them by their past relationship. This is one of the most challenging moments in the adult life of the empath, one that would have a significant impact on their life. But this could all have been avoided had the empath realized early on who they were dealing with and taken the right measures. It is no easy thing to do, knowing a narcissist for who they are, but the following signs should help to give an insight into what they might look and act like.

- **Narcissists would usually threaten you**

If you are in a relationship with someone who constantly threatens you, either to reveal a certain shortcoming of yours or to leave the relationship, you may be with a narcissist. Some of the typical statements by narcissists include:

- ○ "I'll leave this relationship and never look back."

- ○ "I'll reveal the kind of person you really are to everyone" (even if it's not true).

- ○ "You may leave the relationship if you want, I don't need you anyway."

- ○ "Stop this thing you're doing or I will…"

- **Narcissists would try to make you feel guilty**

A true narcissist would try very hard to dig up dirt (particularly from your past), be it true or false, which they can use later to their advantage and your detriment. They leverage the information they have about you that is not particularly good or even true to try to inflict pain upon you. Sometimes they even go to the extent of blaming you for the things they did wrong, putting the blame on you and making you feel as though you're going insane. Furthermore, they try to pin all of your accomplishments to their name, making you look and feel totally dependent on them even if they have done nothing to aid your cause in any way. They say statements like: "You wouldn't have been able to do that without my help," "There is no way on earth you could have pulled that off were it not for my…," and "I'm the reason why you were able to go this far." Narcissists are masters in the art of manipulation. They make you play into their hands, and once you are within their tight grip, you won't have the capacity to think you are worth anything without them.

- **They have an inflated feeling of entitlement**

As a general rule, narcissists are apt to feel superior and entitled. Whenever there are options as to whether their needs should be met instead of yours, they always choose to have their needs met while yours can burn to ash for all they care.

- **They have a solid belief that they are indeed very special**

Have you ever heard your partner say they are some sort of special being or savior? If your partner constantly states and reiterates that they are very special people who others cannot live without, there is a high chance you are in a relationship with a narcissist.

- **They act as though rules are not meant for them and do not necessarily apply to them**

Narcissists act as though they are too important for other people's rules to apply to them in any way. If your partner breaks the queue, always wants to get ahead of others no matter the cost, or disregards laid down rules and regulations, you may be in a relationship with a narcissist.

- **Narcissists are mood-changers**

A narcissist can switch from totally sweet and adorable (even sexually attractive) to utterly cold and scornful in a matter of seconds without any obvious provocation. And what's more, they would try to blame their erratic mood changes on you, of course.

- **They pay too much attention to their external selves**

Narcissists often try to make their little selves big and attractive with external beautification. They buy clothes, own gadgets, pursue careers, make themselves look physically attractive, and push for other material things to mask their true, small selves.

- **They always want to be 'in charge' of the conversation**

Because they can't see beyond themselves, narcissists try to hog the conversation and make it about themselves even when the topic of discussion does not relate to them.

Narcissists have twisted ideologies about what a perfect relationship should be like, and even when they do get into a truly perfect relationship, their only motive is to use the situation to their advantage. Empaths, on the other hand, genuinely love and care about their partners, thus making them the perfect prey for narcissistic predators. A relationship between a narcissist and an empath is almost certain to go awry as time progresses unless the empath is so tolerant that they lose their own voice and identity in the relationship forever (leading to undesirable codependency). If you still want to find your dream relationship and not fall prey to the cold hands of narcissists, it is vital, even crucial, that you take the tips and guidelines herein to heart and act in your own best interests.

MINDFULLNESS AND ADMITTING TO THE PROBLEM IS THE FIRST STEP

A Socratic proverb states that "understanding a question is half the answer" to any particular question. In the same way, knowing that a problem exists is a big step towards solving it. Obviously, you cannot solve a problem whose existence you are not aware of. You might have been wondering if you are codependent, or if the relationship you are having is healthy or normal. In order to be able to assess your relationships effectively, you need to know what exactly is going on in your life and have a deep understanding of who you are.

Caring isn't the problem

As much as being codependent might have caused you a lot of emotional pain and made you feel subdued in your relationship, you need to know that it is not an entirely negative quality. Being codependent doesn't make you altogether bad. The problems you have are not entirely your fault. The people around you, family, friends, and other acquaintances also play a role in them. It is the people around you that probably aided your progress to full-blown codependent status.

Being very caring and empathetic isn't a crime at all. It comes with certain benefits. When not taken to excessive levels, it makes you generous and giving. Your heart is full of love, and you love to see that everyone close to you is happy and not hurt by your actions. You tend to give to others some of your time, resources, and compassion. This can be a wonderful trait that will surely make you loved by others. But when you are in a relationship with a narcissist, this trait may cause you a lot of pain.

Caring gives you the special ability to understand people's emotions and empathy can give you a hint to the emotional state of those around you. You understand people's pain even when they do not say it and tend to be more sensitive to the feelings of others. All you need to do about this is to understand that you do not have an obligation to take away people's pain or make the pain yours always.

As a caring person, you will be reliable; people can count on your support and help when they need it. You are always loyal and willing to be of help. However, you must remember that as much as you want to help others, you need to take care of yourself first. And the people in your life should be able to understand that. You need to understand when you need to draw a line and decline. You have to learn to put yourself first.

In general, what is required of you is not that you get rid of yourself and change who you are. You do not have to let go of the things you are made of and which your family and friends love about you. What you have to do is to understand when your own emotional needs are being neglected or treated poorly because you put the needs of others first. It is okay for you to feel the need to help a friend or a partner in your life. What is not okay is for you to make yourself completely vulnerable because of your desire to please others.

Mindfulness as the first step

Care and concern can quickly degenerate into an emotional fiasco when you lose control of your awareness of them. Most people do things absentmindedly; they even love and relate absentmindedly. When this absentmindedness remains unchecked, negative traits such as codependency show up

To arrest the problem, you need to be aware of it first. Mindfulness comes to the rescue here. In the most basic sense, "Mindfulness" is a state of being fully aware of where you are, and what is happening around you, without losing track or wandering aimlessly in thought. It seems like an easy thing to do, but often, we find ourselves lost and completely unaware of our surroundings. Sometimes, we get lost in thought, and still can't exactly point out what our mind was on, just a few seconds ago. This happens in the absence of mindfulness.

Not only is being mindful about knowing where we are, or what is happening around us; it is also about knowing what is happening in our lives. Many people do not have a genuine idea or clarity about their lives. We do not know how much weight we lose or gain; how much progress we make in school; how our performance is at work; or even how our attitudes and habits affect us and those around us. Most people simply exist without getting a grip on their minds.

The most exciting thing about mindfulness is that it is inherent in us. It is not a trait we have to acquire actively; we just need to know how to make it work. Unless you learn to be mindful of your life, you may find it hard even to decide if you are codependent and empathetic.

For you to be able to fix your codependency and have normal healthy relationships, you need to admit to the fact that you are indeed codependent. You cannot do that unless you become mindful of who you are. This is why mindfulness is such a crucial element in your desire to free yourself.

The Core of Mindfulness

Although mindfulness is an innate quality in us, we need

to learn ways to cultivate it and make it beneficial to us in our lives. It is about building some space for ourselves in our own lives. The following are points you need to remember about mindfulness:

Mindfulness is not an obscure phenomenon: mindfulness has always been in you. It is part of our nature. It is something that you just do not pay attention to. It is not a new skill you need to acquire; it is an inherent ability we need to explore. You do not need to change who you are in order to be mindful. It is not about shutting down your mind; it is about knowing what is happening over there.

No need for change: mindfulness does not need you to become someone else. It is in our nature as humans to resist change. We tend to shy away from anything that will change us even if it will benefit us. You do not have to worry about that with mindfulness. Mindfulness doesn't change who you are; it helps you understand who you are.

Anyone can do it: mindfulness is not something that is reserved for a few experts. It is for everyone. You can do it, as can everyone. It is easy to learn and apply by everyone. So, you do not need to worry about the need for extra expertise or additional skill. The one thing you need is for you to allocate time for practicing your mindfulness skills daily.

Mindfulness is evidence-based: you do not have to

be faithful or religious to benefit from mindfulness. It is not reserved for members of any particular religion or any special sect. Science and experience have proven the benefits that mindfulness has to individuals.

The mind always wanders: most times when you sit for mindfulness meditation, especially in the beginning, you will notice that your mind wanders. It will stray off from your present to some random thoughts in the past. It will do everything it can to take you out of the present. The sooner you get to bring it back on track, the better your mindfulness skills will be. And with time, you will learn to come back to the present sooner than you used to do.

The brain always judges: as you go through your thoughts and actions in your head, your brain will like to judge. However, you need to remember here that your job is not to judge your actions but to be fully mindful and aware of them. So, you do need to neglect any judgmental comment that may pop up in your head and focus rather on being aware of the present.

Pay attention: it may be difficult to ignore distractions and pay attention to little details, especially in this our world of multiple distractions. But paying attention to yourself and your environment helps you become more mindful. When you pay attention, you feel things in a different way and seem to be able to connect with all your senses- smell, taste, touch, sound, and sight. Paying attention to your thoughts, actions, and feelings will help you in being mindful of your codependent nature and set you on the right track to freeing yourself from it.

Live in the moment: live through every moment in your life. Try to focus your attention on everything you do and be mindful of it. This way, you will be able to notice the codependent nature of your actions and how they affect you. Besides, it will also help you enjoy the little things you have always overlooked.

Accept yourself: accept yourself the way you are. That you are codependent doesn't make you a bad or horrible person. Treat yourself the way you treat your friends and loved ones. You deserve some love too.

Focus on your breath: focus on your breath a lot. It helps you in being mindful. Focusing on your breathing makes you more aware of yourself and helps you clear your thoughts. Follow your breath as it goes in and out. Human brains are naturally designed to stray in thought unless you hold yourself to mindful existence. Focusing on your thoughts helps you live in the present and brings you back from your random thoughts.

Mindfulness Meditation

Once you practice mindfulness, you will be able to realize how much you have been codependent. You will recall clearly all the times in your life when you have put the needs of others before your own needs at your own detriment. You will become actively aware of how you have been scared of losing the approval of so many people at the expense of your own identity. You will get to know why you must strive to get rid of your codependency and become independent and confident.

One of the most efficient and proven techniques that helps with mindfulness is meditation. In mindfulness meditation, you try to become intensely aware of your thoughts and feelings at a particular moment without judgment or interpretation. Mindfulness meditation can be achieved through walking, moving, standing, or seated meditation. It gives us time to explore ourselves and understand our true nature. Meditation starts with the body. For you to be aware of your mind, you first have to be aware of your body. Meditation gives you that chance of being intimately conscious of what is happening to your body and mind. These meditation exercises help relax the brain and body and relieve stress; these in turn help in opening up our mind and understanding.

A Simple Mindfulness Meditation Technique

- Sit in a quiet place where there are no moving distractions in front of you.

- Sit in a relaxed pose that has your back straight and comfortable.

- Now, take in a deep breath. Trace the path of the breath you have taken in.

- Note the physical changes that breathing brings; the expansion of your diaphragm and filling up of the lungs are important.

- Now, hold your breath for about five seconds.

- Slowly exhale the breath.

- Allow your mind to roam all over you as you exhale, noting the physical changes.

- If your mind wanders outside your exercise, gently recall your mind and return.

- Remain in this posture for ten to fifteen minutes every day.

Mindfulness gives you the power to observe your entire life and character profile without being judgmental. It gradually calls your attention to everything that is wrong and gives you time to fix it. It is your first tool of awareness in the battle to be rid of too much empathy and codependency.

THE POWER OF HEALTHY RELATIONSHIPS

A healthy relationship is one of the vital ingredients of a healthy life. However, a healthy relationship is not the same as a perfect relationship, as the latter does not exist. A healthy relationship is a relationship that, overall, makes you feel good about yourself and about the person with whom you are in a relationship. The role of any relationship is to enrich our lives and help us create memories we would be happy to keep. Therefore, a relationship that fulfills this underlying principle can be sincerely said to be a healthy one, and any relationship that goes against this basic tenet is an unhealthy one. Apart from improving the quality of your life, building and sustaining a healthy relationship has the capacity to also speed up the recovery process due in part to the fact that it can help people in recovery get the motivation and support that they need to stay sober.

As humans, we have a certain tendency to want to associate with one another. This is an inevitable truth and is one that pushes us to relate with the people we come across. In relating to these people, we create different kinds of relationships, such as familial relationships, social relationships, romantic relationships, and professional relationships. These different kinds of relationship offer different value propositions, operate differently to one another, and are all highly vital for personal development and mental healing.

Both healthy and unhealthy relationships can influence and impact your life in various ways. While the effects of the relationships you keep can be quite pronounced and obvious, sometimes these effects are subtle and stay beneath the surface of your perception. Depending on whether you are in a good relationship or a bad one, these effects either nurture your mind or corrode it. If, for example, you are suffering from an addiction and are on the verge of a full recovery following therapy, a supportive friend who truly cares for you would offer you support and motivate you to remain sober while an unsupportive, toxic friend would throw jibes at you for having an addiction. While you may laugh over the mockery that your unsupportive friend makes about your addiction (because you think that's what friends do), it does damage to your mental health, with or without you knowing it. In order to find and keep healthy relationships, you need to put in conscious efforts to recognize unhealthy relationships. Only by distinguishing between healthy and unhealthy relationships will you be able to rid your life of unhealthy relationships and cultivate healthy ones.

Differentiating Between Healthy and Unhealthy Relationships

To be able to tell healthy and unhealthy relationships apart, you must know the tell-tale signs of healthy relationships. These signs include empathy, feeling valued, respect, support, stability, compromise, commitment, loyalty, effective communication, trust, affection, honesty, connection, safety, security, comfort, attention, understanding, and soothing feeling. These and many more signs are inherent in a healthy relationship.

While all of these traits are important signs of a healthy relationship, four of them – understanding, security, safety, and soothing feeling – are some of the most crucial of them, and will, therefore, be discussed further.

- **Every healthy relationship must have understanding**; that is, the people in the relationship must be able to understand each other's behaviors. Even though it's not possible to always understand a person you're in a relationship with, it is always worthwhile to try. Everyone wants to be seen and understood, and if your partner sees that you are putting in conscious efforts to understand them, they feel more valued, and that inexplicably affects the relationship positively. In this light, the person with whom you are in a relationship must show signs that they are trying to understand your actions and inactions. They must encourage and motivate you to go on and be supportive when you are in your trying moments. They must, in essence, see the world through your eyes, for that is the only pathway to true understanding. When in disagreement, your partner should be able to understand your views and opinions better and hence know the reasons behind your words and actions if they have learned to see things from your viewpoint. Codependent relationships suffer from a lack of general understanding. Both parties do not understand each other. They simply take the rough road out and hope for the best.

- **A sense of security is paramount for a healthy relationship**; and since our lives are significantly influenced by the relationships we keep, it is vital for us to feel secure in our relationships. Security is a sense of safety coupled with stability; it gives us the feeling that our partners are there for us through thick and thin, and will be there to hold our hands through the ups and downs of the relationship. A codependent individual may hold unfounded fears that destabilize his mental state and make it less likely for him/her to hold a fruitful, mutually-satisfying relationship.

- **It's a no-brainer that one needs to be in a state of safety in a relationship**. It can be argued that emotional safety is just as important as physical safety for a healthy relationship. For you to consider your relationship healthy, you and your partner must have created an atmosphere of serenity where you talk in gentle tones and treat each other with respect. If your partner is not treating you this way, then your relationship may not be safe, nor is it healthy. You must pay attention to the words and actions of your partner to find out exactly how safe your relationship is. Notice the difference between "I" and "You" statements and assess how you feel about them. For example, there is a difference between "You need to be doing more chores around the house" and "Honey, the house chores are becoming overwhelming for me. I'll appreciate some help." Which of these statements are you likely to respond to better? With respect to codependency and empathy, healthy relationships reduce the amount of physical and emotional stress each partner has to face.

- **A healthy relationship is soothing to our inner environments**. In fact, it has been proven that physical pain registers less when our hand is held by a loving and caring partner. In contrast, pain registers more severely when a partner with whom we are in an unhappy relationship holds our hand.

Any relationship that isn't safe, secure, doesn't soothe your mind, or doesn't make room for understanding is not healthy, simple as that.

Telltale Signs of An Unhealthy Relationship

A healthy relationship gives room for growth and is self-sustaining, meaning struggles within the relationship can be resolved by the people in the relationship, without the input of external forces or people. An unhealthy relationship, on the other hand, is toxic and usually inhibitory. It cripples you and intoxicates your thoughts and emotions. It is rife with grief and is always self-destructive. An unhealthy relationship is bad for your physical, mental, and emotional wellbeing, and can reduce the quality of one's life in general. In order to be able to get out of an unhealthy relationship, you must first be able to identify one. Here are ten telltale signs of an unhealthy relationship:

- **Excessive possessiveness:** It is absolutely essential that you and your partner are aware of the fact, and even go to the length of telling each other, that you are theirs and they are yours. However, when taken to the extreme, it could be a sign of one partner not trusting the other enough. If your partner is distrusting and extremely possessive, they might tell you things like "I don't trust you" or "I don't like you talking to him/her." In fact, in extreme situations, a possessive partner may try to isolate you from the people you love or people you would normally relate with, especially those who know you are in an unhealthy relationship and who would try to talk you out of being with your partner.

- **Neglecting or disrespecting boundaries:** The power and importance of setting boundaries in a relationship cannot be overemphasized and cannot be covered in this text at this time. Boundaries help partners relate well with each other while making sure that they respect each other's individuality, accept it, and let each other exhibit it. A healthy relationship would normally have boundaries that are recognized and respected by the parties involved. An unhealthy relationship, in contrast, does not respect the significance of and therefore does not make room for boundaries. If your partner does not respect your boundaries, he is apt to encroach your comfort zone, and that would most certainly upset you. Furthermore, if your partner neglects your boundaries, it simply means that your needs are not as important as his, and that respect for your self-worth is not very valuable to him.

- **Your partner exhibits controlling behavior:** Your partner can control your life on several fronts – emotionally, mentally, financially, and physically. It is alright for your partner to try to help or assist you in handling certain tasks, but when your partner always tries to tell you what to do in an assertive and controlling manner, it's a sign that they may not believe you have the capacity to handle anything on your own. In a financial control situation, for example, your partner may try to restrict your access to your own money or try to tell you which job to take and which one to quit or let go. And they don't do this purely as an act of helping you to make better decisions; rather they do so to demonstrate that they have a tight grip on your financial life and can, therefore, assert their control. Physical control can come in the form of your partner telling you where you can or can't go, or checking the GPS system in your car to find out where you have gone.

- **Aggressive behavior:** Being on the receiving end of aggressive behavior from your partner is perhaps one of the most traumatic things anyone could ever face in a relationship. Contrary to what many people believe, aggressive behavior does not need to involve a physical action or touch; it could be in the form of your partner punching the air or wall, throwing or smashing objects, breaking things, or destroying items. Do not be fooled by your partner shrugging off their aggressive behavior as play-fighting or trying to make you feel the same. It is reported that most aggressors exhibit aggressive behavior to show the other party that they have control or strength over them. So, pay attention to your relationship and watch out for any of these aggressive behaviors. Sure, everyone gets angry sometimes, and even the calmest of people sometimes throw a vase or two, but when it becomes all too often, you should certainly begin to look at their behavior under a different, more discerning lens. Another sign of aggressive behavior is forced sex. It is not normal or healthy for your partner to force you to have sex with them, even if they had organized an expensive dinner. Apart from using physical force, your partner may also try to manipulate you into having sex with them by using guilt trips or threatening to leave the relationship.

- **Secretiveness:** Even the healthiest of relationships have secrets, things that are better kept away from each other. However, it is unhealthy for your partner to resort to telling lies or keeping vital information from your knowledge. Too many secrets can destroy the very fabric of a relationship – safety and security. It is a different case if you and your partner have decided to keep certain things away from each other, such as the things you discuss or encounter at your place of work, what you both do on weekends if either of you is out of town, or your previous relationships. This is totally healthy. However, if you prefer transparency in your relationship and your partner is too secretive, then there is a problem at hand.

- **Your partner ignores you when you need them:** A trend that has proven very effective over time in relationships is one partner ignoring the other or giving the other the silent treatment when they know the other person needs their help. Additionally, if you are in pain or in need of some urgent help – regardless of what has happened between you and your partner in the past – and your partner is apathetic or ignores you like you don't matter, then you may be in an unhealthy relationship. Your partner must always pay attention to your needs, no matter the present situation between you both.

- **Use of gaslighting:** Gaslighting is a term used to describe a situation where a partner uses brainwashing on the other to undermine their sanity or the reality of the situation around them. Gaslighting is a significant form of abuse that detracts from a victim's emotional wellbeing. If your partner uses gaslighting to escape from a situation or absolve themselves of guilt, then you are certainly in an unhealthy relationship.

- **Unpredictability or mood swings:** It is perfectly normal for partners in a relationship to have minor fights every now and then, even if one partner appears to be clearly more incensed than the other. However, unpredictable, unreasonable, sudden explosions are neither normal nor healthy. Sometimes partners who suddenly explode over little matters pin their blowups as a sign of their passion, but do not be swayed by this excuse. It could indeed be an early sign that you are in an unhealthy relationship. If the sudden blow-ups are usually accompanied by abusive language and/or action, then there is certainly a serious cause for concern.

- **Too much worrying:** Every person wants to be loved and cared about by their partner, of course. And with love and care comes the need to feel worried about your significant other. It is normal, even good, for your partner to worry about you. However, when this worrying becomes excessive in the sense that your partner gets irritated or irate when you don't text them back immediately or return their calls within five minutes of receiving them, then you may be in for an unhealthy relationship. If this is the case, your freedom and sense of independence slowly corrode as you succumb to your partner's excessive demands.

- **Your partner does not say they are sorry:** After an argument or fight one of the most reasonable things to do is apologize for the part you played in the misunderstanding. If your partner refuses to say sorry after an argument, you should not immediately start to think that you're wrong and they are in the right. If you do this, they might take advantage of the situation, and you may have plunged yourself into an abusive relationship. Furthermore, if you always apologize after an argument (unless, of course, you're always the one making trouble), you make your partner unable to be introspective enough to assess what they can change or improve about themselves. Hence, they get a mindset that you are always wrong, and they are always right, no matter what the facts and figures show.

Essential Relationship Tips

You must be willing and able to discern between a healthy and unhealthy relationship. If you do assess your relationship and find out that it is abusive or unhealthy, then you would have finished the first step of the process. If your relationship has not yet reached the point of no return and you still feel what you have, can be salvaged, then here are ten tips to help you get your relationship working again and better than ever:

- **Speak up and speak truly:** As trivial as this sounds, so many relationships suffer from a sheer lack of verbal communication. You cannot possibly expect your partner to be able to read your mind (it may not even be in your best interest for them to) or figure out what it is you are thinking or feeling. If there is something you feel your partner needs to hear about, be sure to communicate it to them in clear terms. In the same vein, if there is something your partner is doing that harms you or makes you uncomfortable, be sure to tell them about it; you would have taken the all-important first step towards solving the issue. Sometimes your failure to speak up can make problems fester and become worse over time. In speaking up, ensure you are respectful and modest. You don't want your partner thinking that you don't value or respect them; that's a major conversation killer.

- **Listen carefully:** A very important ingredient of a healthy relationship is to know when to put your voice out and when to listen. You must put in conscious efforts to not interrupt your partner when they are talking but rather, allow them to finish expressing their thoughts. Don't allow yourself to get caught up in the dark web of trying to fashion a response to what your partner is saying, while they are still speaking; listen intently. Even if you don't agree with what your partner is saying, you must still be attentive and respect the fact that they have something to say. Cutting your partner off in their speech only serves to worsen the situation, and could make them do the same to you. On the flip side, if your partner has a history of interrupting you when you are talking, you could respectfully demand that they allow you to finish your speech before they begin theirs.

- **Show concern:** Even if you have fallen out with your partner, whether recently or a long time ago, you may still find yourself showing concern for them if they are going through a rough patch. You must be able to show your partner that you are concerned about their wellbeing at any point in time, regardless of the present situation, if you want yours to be a healthy relationship. Showing concern for your partner's state of affairs is a way of telling them that you still care and that you still have their best interests at heart. Showing that you care could elicit a positive reaction in your partner and make them show concern for you as well.

- **Create healthy boundaries:** Boundaries are a vital part of a healthy relationship. They are not meant to make you or your partner feel trapped, but to ensure that there is respect in the relationship. If your partner has a habit of doing something that makes you feel uneasy or uncomfortable, bring it up and discuss it with them, stating how you would rather they behaved. For instance, if your partner has developed a habit of entering the bathroom while you are in it without knocking, and that makes you uncomfortable, talk about it with them. Create a boundary that discourages that action and get your security. On your own part, you must respect your partner's boundaries always and at all cost. Do not ask for your partner's social media login details or read their messages. You must learn to respect the lines they have drawn by staying on the safe side of it. Additionally, you could create social boundaries by telling your partner that you would like to have a night per week to yourself to hang out with friends and family. A major thing to note here is to ensure that you don't set out to control your partner with your boundaries or get controlled by your partner with theirs. Most importantly, do not cross any boundary to offer your help.

- **Share your feelings:** Don't be afraid to share your feelings with your partner. Always state clearly how you are feeling and make gestures that go in tandem with your present state. Also, try to show an interest in the way your partner is feeling and be sure to support and be of assistance to them in their times of need. When you connect with your partner on an emotional level, you're sure to empathize with them more and understand their experience better. If you feel that there is an emotional disconnection between you and your partner, make inquiries about their feelings (and do so without being judgmental or subjective). Try to be as objective as possible and understand things from their own points of view.

- **Discuss the relationship with your partner:** Make out time to check in with your partner and discuss the trajectory of your relationship. You must make an effort (and implore your partner) to make time for helpful conversations. You could discuss your relationship goals, expectations, and aspirations, for example. If you ignore the need to have a conversation with your partner – especially about difficult matters – you might be heading towards an unhealthy relationship.

- **Ground your relationship in respect:** Many relationships that go sour used to be all sweet and cozy. Some of these relationships became extremely abusive and eventually broke apart because their foundations were not rooted in mutual respect. You must respect your partner at all times and speak and act in ways that demand the same level of respect from them. Make it a rule that even in stressful situations, you would never treat each other without respect. That way, you can have arguments without resorting to the use of abusive language or exhibiting aggressive behavior. Respecting your partner means that you value their thoughts, emotions, feelings, speech, and actions. It means that you don't engage in name-calling or any other act that can endanger the respect in the relationship.

- **Appreciate your partner and be appreciated by them:** One of the telltale signs of a healthy relationship is appreciation between partners. Endeavor to appreciate the little and big things that your partner does for you. Sometimes a simple "thank you" can show that you are appreciative of your partner's efforts. Appreciating your partner makes them feel valued and makes them think that their time and efforts matter. Same goes for you as well. If you don't feel appreciated in your relationship, tell your partner about how you would love to be appreciated. You could tell them, "I feel appreciated when you say 'thank you' for the things I do for you."

- **Spend time together:** With technology seemingly taking over the realm of communication in the modern era, it is easy to have long chats with your partner yet say so little to each other face-to-face. It is possible for you both to set up a digital fundraiser yet do very little together physically. Face-to-face communication is better than anything social media or telecommunications can offer because sometimes the nonverbal attributes of a person can add a world of meaning to the words they say. Spending quality time with your partner serves to improve the bond between you and bolster your emotional points.

- **Let go of codependence:** Your codependent behavior, contrary to what you might believe, does not help improve the attitude of the person with whom you are in a relationship. Instead, you only help enable their irresponsible behavior, further putting yourself at a disadvantage. If you are trapped in codependency, you may struggle to stop yourself from enabling your partner's inappropriate behavior simply because you have imprinted it on your mind that you cannot ever say "no" to them and would rather go silent than saying something that would start a fight. You must identify the codependence behaviors you are exhibiting and try to improve them either personally or with the help of a therapist.

Building an Interdependent Relationship

When you realize that you are an empath and/or codependent, only then can you begin to understand clearly the reality of your situation and how to tackle it. As humans, we are bound to want to connect with others on an emotional level, meaning that we are, to an extent, dependent or reliant on another person's emotional response to us. However, when this dependence or reliance becomes exaggerated, then there is a serious problem that must be subdued. Such is the life of an empath or codependent.

If you are codependent, chances are you have little to

no sense of self-valuation and have learned to depend on the views of others, especially those you are in an emotional relationship with, for approval and appreciation. However, like normal, everyday people, empaths, and codependents have positive expectations from their relationships. Like other people, they want a loving, wonderful, lifelong relationship with the person they deem is the most important person in their lives. The bitter truth is that empaths and codependents do not always get this dream relationship. Some empaths and codependents are lucky enough to get into happy relationships and fulfill their relationship goals, but then others get unfortunately hooked to narcissists, and they get the worst nightmares of their lives.

Now, what is the solution to codependence and dependence in relationships? The answer is interdependence.

Interdependence is a term that is used to describe a situation in a relationship where partners recognize the existence of and respect each other's feelings as well as the emotional bond that exists between them, whilst at the same time acknowledging and maintaining their individual sense of self. Hence, an interdependent partner knows the essence of vulnerability and is not afraid to demand and create emotional intimacy between themselves and their partners. At the same time, the interdependent partner also recognizes the fact that they are different from their partner and hence is able to accommodate their partner's individuality without compromising their own individuality, belief systems, or core values.

In interdependent relationships, the goal is on thriving off each other's efforts without asking for more than what your partner can provide. Interdependent relationships are made up of two individuals who are aware of their responsibilities and are willing to pick them and execute them. In interdependence, both partners are on the same wavelength and moving in the same direction. The pace is set mutually and followed hand-in-hand.

No matter how you look at it, being emotionally dependent on another person, be them your partner, family, or friend, does not bode well for you on any level. Dependence often creates an unhealthy atmosphere in a relationship and eventually leads to one partner taking advantage of the other partner's dependence to their detriment. On a similar note, total independence does not solve the problem of codependence. Independence, when taken to the extreme, can lead to an emotional disconnection between partners and restrict the growth of their relationship. If you feel overly independent, you may begin to feel that intimacy with your partner is not essential for the health of your relationship; it is difficult for any progress to occur in this situation. Because of this reason, independence is not recommended as a way of dealing with codependence or empathy.

Interdependence is different from codependence. A codependent individual is apt to depend on others for their own sense of self-approval and wellbeing. Hence, for this individual, it is difficult to draw a bold line between their individuality and their partner's approval. A codependent relationship would usually have poor or no boundaries, people-pleasing attitude, poor communication, extreme sensitivity, manipulation, blame game, low self-esteem, and a lack of goal-setting beyond the extent of the relationship. This type of relationship is not healthy and does not create a room for individual partners to exhibit their true character and be themselves.

On the other hand, an interdependent relationship strives to strike a balance between individual partners' sense of self and shared bond within the relationship. It understands that each partner is trying earnestly to be there for the other partner and is working sincerely to meet the emotional and physical demands of their significant other. In an interdependent relationship, no partner demands too much of the other partner, and neither of them looks to the other for a sense of self-worth or approval. This allows either partner enough room to be themselves and exhibit their true nature while still paying attention to the shared needs, expectations, and goals of the relationship. Interdependent partners tend to communicate clearly, set and respect each other's healthy boundaries, listen to each other actively and attentively, create time to fulfill the relationship's needs, take responsibility for their behaviors, are not afraid to let their fears and vulnerabilities known, have healthy self-esteem levels, engage with and respond well to each other, and are open to and approachable by each other.

You must strive to build an interdependent relationship as a long-lasting remedy to your ailing codependent relationship, way before your relationship crumbles and falls apart. A vital factor in building an interdependent relationship is to be aware of who you are right at the onset of the relationship. Sometimes people enter into relationships for the wrong reasons – so they can avoid being alone, so they have someone to wake up to every morning, and other wrong reasons – and in so doing they do not take cognizance of who they are, what their belief systems are, what core values they have, or what they truly want in a relationship. Take time to introspect and ask yourself who you are and what you stand for. Ask yourself what relationship goals you would like to set and achieve. This allows you to venture into a relationship with solid knowledge of self; this knowledge is a crucial ingredient for building an interdependent relationship. If you are having a hard time resonating with your sense of self, perhaps the following tips would be of help:

- Have knowledge of what exactly you want in a relationship and what matters to you.
- Do not be scared to demand what you want in a relationship; you deserve the perfect relationship, and there is no reason why you should ever settle for less.
- Make time outside of your relationship to spend quality time with friends and family.
- Do not lose track of your personal goals. It's alright for your attention to shift from your personal to your relationship goals from time to time, but ensure to always remind yourself of what your personal goals are, and endeavor to work towards achieving them.
- Don't forget or compromise your core values and beliefs.
- Get some hobbies and make time to exercise them.
- Get grounded in the habit of saying "no" when it is necessary to say.
- Don't undermine yourself to please others. Remember that you matter too.

As you aim to be more mindful of yourself, be sure to allow your partner to do the same, as that would establish a healthy environment in which an interdependent relationship can thrive and blossom.

EMPATH EMOTIONS AND HOW TO BLOCK OUT OTHERS' DISTRESS

There are many definitions of who an empath is, and what empathy entails; from metaphysical ramifications to neurological evidence. However, the unifying thread for all of these schools of thought is that empaths are "highly sensitive," and empaths are all able to "feel.'

As an empath, your life is determined, controlled, and characterized by a wide range of emotions. Unharnessed, you are swayed by every nuance, and cadence in the tones of voices you hear. Like a proverbial victor, this eventually turns you into a victim. Every single minute of the day, you remain intuitive and perceptive to energy flow in your environment, and highly susceptible to the resulting effects. I refer to this as "shedding more tears than the bereaved." Being intuitive means that you are extra-aware of even veiled moments of sadness, excitement, grief, and panic.

Think of it this way. Every action we perform and our mood combine to emit energy at a certain frequency. The general rule of thumb is that the higher the frequency at which an emotion is emitted, the more likely it is for the people around the source to pick it up. Feel depressed, and you emit low energy at a very low-frequency level. Get super-excited, and you are throwing energy darts at everyone around. That is why it is easy to get infected by emotions and actions such as happiness and laughter. Negative emotions can also emit energy at high frequencies. For instance, panic is one of the most infectious emotions around.

How do these energy levels and frequencies affect the average man? Have you ever walked into a room and it felt as if the air was heavy? Did you then proceed to sit down quietly and remain apprehensive? In cases like these, you got infected by the frequencies of the people already in the room. You received them, and they modulated your own energy to match theirs. By the same rule, you can get whipped into a frenzy by simply listening to a speech or podcast. As humans, the rule is that our energy levels and frequencies are affected by both the average energy level of the people closest to us, and the energy level of those in our current environment. It is the way we get to share emotions at all.

However, the rate at which we pick up these energy emissions differs markedly from individual to individual. Some people can literally remain in a boiling teapot and remain calm. Empaths are so highly attuned that they pick up every emission as it is made. They not only pick up energy; they imbibe and dissolve under the pressure of taking in different energy emissions all at once. That is the source of the energy drain they experience.

Being able to key into other people, and even perform a bit of telepathy is not entirely a blessing if you do not learn to control it. In fact, most times, empaths suffer their ability as a curse because they groan under the weight of the information overload and the signals they are picking up. Nature has made most humans with a high threshold for detecting energy. So, as a defensive ideal, typical humans do not pick up energy easily. That is different from empaths who pick up everything.

Without a filter for sieving out unneeded energy, empaths run afoul of a lot of mental traffic laws that ensure that they are constantly in a state of changing emotions. Most empaths, therefore, frequently become sad, depressed, stressed, and dejected at the snap of a finger. This is because they absorb energy when their friends are upset. They receive energy when an animal is hurt even. Primed, and sensitive, it is imperative for you as an empath to avoid emotional exhaustion.

Avoiding Emotional Exhaustion as An Empath

Life can be so exhausting for an empath that has not trained himself in the art of acceptance and detachment. However, the following steps can help you keep mental exhaustion to the barest minimum.

- **Eliminate your stressors**

For empaths, it is important to know that while many things may trigger emotional exhaustion, the causative factor of emotional exhaustion is often the 'individual or the object' of our thought. If you have people giving out toxic energy around you that you pick up, you will experience more incidents of stress, burnouts, headaches, and tiredness. Especially while you are still attempting to recover, you will remain susceptible to wrong energy. The prudent thing to do is to distance yourself from known stressors that get you under all the time. Each time, you go through avoidable pain, you etch it deeper into your consciousness. Every time you avoid it, you give yourself a better chance at controlling your own energy levels.

- **Exercise more**

Psychologists and counselors often advise empaths to try different forms of exercise as they pack limitless potential for boosting your mood and ensuring you stay mentally fit. Do not get browbeaten into becoming a recluse on account of your sensitivity as an empath. Exercise releases an ample supply of hormones such as endorphins, adrenaline, and dopamine, which can make you feel good and lift you. In addition, exercise improves cognition, mental awareness, and increases your perseverance limits.

- **Employ mindfulness**

You can always identify an empath, especially one struggling with emotional exhaustion, if you step into a room and you are casually observant. Empaths are always lost in contemplation; empaths are always engrossed in one thought or another, which makes them unable to enjoy the present. If you are constantly drained by the amount of energy you absorb from the environment, then one way to deal with this is yoga and different mindfulness exercises. Divide your day into bits where you can practice guided meditation. You can use meditation apps if you are always on the run.

- **Use sleep to wind down**

Empaths may suffer from insomnia, especially when they are overstimulated. This insomnia may carry through even when the stimulating source is removed. Aside from that, think of sleep as a manual reset button allowing you to recoup your energy and start afresh. Most counselors will advise that you establish a regular sleep routine to ensure that you are recharging your batteries. Sleep helps you keep negative vibes away and out of your mind.

- **Change your environment if possible**

Empaths generally treasure peaceful and natural environments where they can be in their own skin and enjoy the moment. By extension, certain other environments do more harm than good. Being in certain scenes may set off your empathetic alarm clock even without any visible stressor present. It is a two-step process to ensure that you avoid emotional stress, and this includes identifying and changing the environments that don't suit you.

- **Seek therapy**

Therapy is a chapter on its own later in this book, but it has to be mentioned. Being too sensitive is not a condition you may be able to treat on your own. You improve your chances by seeking and adhering to therapeutic advice from experienced counselors and psychotherapists. No matter how understanding your friends, family, or close circle of associates are, they may not be equipped to help you as an empath in moments of emotional exhaustion. Friends, families, and colleagues may even avoid you as an empath at these moments because they lack two essential qualities: experience and expertise. These two all-important and elusive qualities are the qualities most professionals, like yoga instructors, counselors, and mentors, have in quantum. You need to visit any of these well-trained professionals as they have the experience you lack and the expertise you desperately need to cope with such moments. I happen to know that even speaking about the way I felt as an empath to fellow empaths lifted some of the psychological burdens that the trait placed on me.

- **Avoid drugs, alcohol, and addictive substances**

At the height of my teen years and early adulthood, I was addicted to every drug and substance that I could lay my hands on. In fact, I nearly lost my life after I overdosed. During this period, like many other addicts, I tried to wean myself off chemical dependence, but it was not to be. The level of pain I allowed myself to bear simply required that I lose myself in chemical-fueled hazes. I sought refuge from myself in drugs and alcohol, and the results were as disastrous as could have been predicted.

A lot of empaths fall into this same familiar mistake of resorting to drugs, alcohol, and other addictive substances when they are emotionally exhausted. Like all forms of addiction, alcohol and drugs provide very temporary relief to the individual. They do not resolve the underlying problems or actually alleviate any of the real symptoms.

The mind-altering effects of psychoactive drugs, alcohol, and other intoxicants will only worsen your state. Ensure that you steer clear of drugs, alcohol, and other addictive substances. They shouldn't be taken at all if you can help it.

- **Prepare your mind**

Seeing as you are extremely hypersensitive, and possess an innate tendency to absorb energy unknowingly, you need to rebuild your mind and retrain it to serve as a buffer against the energy onslaught you are going to face as an empath. To avoid being emotionally-drained all the time, an empath must learn to train his mind to focus on positives rather than negatives. You must learn to be grounded and master your emotions. The process of preparing the mind always takes time, patience, and the help of a therapist, but it is definitely worth the while.

- **Learn the art of energy transmutation**

Transmutation is a vital mechanism that can help you defeat emotional exhaustion. Think of it this way. Since you are liable to absorb energy from the people around you, transmutation gives you the chance to convert that energy into a more positive form and expend it too. There is a limit to the amount of energy a human body can absorb without expending it. When you exceed this level, it leads to exhaustion. You can avoid this exhaustion by engaging in activities such as journaling, singing, and other activities that lead to cathartic transmutation.

How to Set Boundaries as an Empath

Most empaths implode and explode because they take in emotions way beyond their natural capacity. With poorly-defined mental barriers, you allow everyone to waltz into your private space and plant their own thoughts and emotions within your mind. You cannot allow this to go on, unchecked. You need to clearly mark out the limits you are willing to go to and confirm that they are safe enough. You need to love yourself within these limits and refuse anything that tasks your limits and drags you out of these bounds. Here are a few ways to ensure you have and protect your emotional boundaries.

• Love yourself most

Loving yourself is the first requirement if you are looking to set tested and trusted boundaries. You need to understand that you are your first priority and your own responsibility. You need to acknowledge that you are a distinct entity separate from all other people. This is the basis for loving yourself and ensuring that you do not collapse under the weight of the emotions you pick up. Not all situations demand your attention or require you to tune in. You can choose to observe happenings without getting immersed by being mindful of your own limits.

• Be selective

For as long as you remain an empath, you will constantly receive mental stimuli and outflow of energy directed towards you. You cannot simply ignore them; they will keep hammering away at your armor till they find a way in. Instead, you need to be selective of what you pick to immerse yourself in. Do not just tune into any energy around and make it yours. Be selective with what emotions you choose to mirror. Be selective of the company you keep and those you invest your time in. For instance, if necessary, do not watch the news regularly or surf social media when you are feeling particularly vulnerable. You are bound to run into sad news or emotion-draining situations if you do. In short, limit your contact with draining incidents and events.

- **Learn to say 'no'**

No empath loves saying 'no' to people as they are scared of the emotions it will cause within the people they say it to. So, typically, we spend the greater part of our lives as people-pleasers. A true empath does not want to be the source of any form of sorrow or sadness in anybody. So, he holds out an olive branch each time to appease everyone. However, this is a guaranteed recipe for disaster.

You may not like to rock the boat, but what if that means you end up at the bottom of the sea when you can no longer cope with the storms. You need to have a "No" so your "yes" can make any meaning. Do not tap into the emotions of the people around needlessly. Do not make the grief of other people yours without being called to help. You need to be able to tune out when needed.

- **Seek balance**

Someone once said that "the greatest law of the universe is the law of balance." That rule applies here also. In setting boundaries as an empath, it is vital to be balanced and not move from one extreme to the other. Setting boundaries does not mean separation, cruelty, and selfishness should creep in. No! Rather, learn to prioritize.

- **Eliminate negativity**

One of the advantages of setting clear boundaries is that you will be able to see the distinct difference between negative and positive energy. You can then plan your day to limit your exposure to the harbingers of negative energy. As an example, do not stand around that pessimistic friend of yours who is forever spewing negative ideas and thoughts. Limit your contact with such sources of negativity.

Empathy is a loss of control over your emotions and the visual cues fed to your brain. To regain control, you must avoid mental exhaustion while setting the right kinds of boundaries to keep out unwanted energy flow.

HOW TO DRAW BOUNDARIES AND COME FACE TO FACE WITH YOUR FEARS

The last chapter dealt with boundaries in an emotional and mental context. In this chapter, we will be dealing with the building and enforcement of boundaries in your relationships to enable you to deal with your codependent nature better.

As a codependent, not only do you need to set boundaries in your life, you also need to preserve those boundaries. You have to make sure that those boundaries are respected and that you get the treatment you really deserve in your relationship. However, before you set boundaries, you need to understand what they are and why you need them.

A boundary literally means a line that signifies limits or marks the end of something. In relationships, boundaries are the limits you set, the things you cannot handle because they may be harmful to you or because you do not like being treated that way. The major cause of problems to codependents in an abusive relationship is a lack of boundaries. They fail to understand the lines that divide them and others. They fail to recognize where they end and where their partner begins.

Everything is blurry to them, and they fall prey to a lot of emotional and physical abuse. If you are codependent, then take this as a warning— unless you wake up today, and set some boundaries for yourself, you will always remain where you are, stuck in a relationship that does more harm than good to you. You need to understand that setting boundaries doesn't mean you are rude. It just means that you are considering your own needs and putting yourself first. It means you have acknowledged the fact that you have neglected your own emotional needs for too long and you are now trying to make amends.

In most cases, the lack of boundaries arises from the problems we faced in childhood. When parents do a poor job of helping their children set good boundaries early in life, they tend to grow up as adults with a poor sense of 'self' and very little or no boundaries at all. They absorb all sort of abuse and unfair treatment because they do not understand the need for them to set boundaries. Developing boundaries will make you understand the different roles you and your partner should play in your relationship. It will help you avoid getting frustrated because you feel you are being trampled upon. It will make you understand when to get up and say no

If you are a codependent who has been in an abusive or narcissistic relationship, then you have to set healthy boundaries. As much as you need boundaries in your life, you have to understand the boundaries you should have. Boundaries should not be too loose, or they may be as good as not being there. Loose boundaries make you accommodate more than you should and keep you prone to the same narcissism or abuse that you are trying to get away from. On the other hand, rigid boundaries will distance you from others and make you feel lonely in your relationships.

The whole idea of setting boundaries is to enable you to have healthy relationships without you succumbing so much to the needs of others that you lose yourself in the process. It is about striking a balance between your needs and those of your partner. It is about recognizing your own self-worth and value.

Dealing with fear

Why do most people maintain weak or porous boundaries? The number one reason is **fear** — fear of the unknown and a chronic lack of self-esteem.

Therefore, before you would be able to set boundaries in your life, you have to face your fears. Fears have always been the reason why codependents find it difficult to set boundaries. Whether it is the fear of losing the partner, of asking too much or being too demanding, you will have to face and overcome them before you will be able to set healthy boundaries. Below are some crucial points that will help you overcome your fears, and get you started on the road to building new boundaries.

• Fear can be overcome

As real as fear feels, it is something you can get rid of. The fears that you have always carried in your heart that have made you endure so much pain are not things you have to live with forever. As much as those fears feel like an integral part of your existence, you can do away with them and get the things that need to be done in your life done for good. You can get out of the narcissistic or abusive relationship you have always been scared of leaving because of your fear about the outcome. The worst relationships are those based on fear — for yourself and of being yourself.

• Accept your fears

To overcome your fears, you have to accept them and realize that you have them. You cannot solve a problem whose existence you have failed to recognize. You also have to acknowledge the negative effects that those fears are having on your life, and how they have prevented you from having normal relationships because you have failed to set boundaries on your life.

Accepting your fears should not make you feel inferior— it is a necessary step towards overcoming those fears.

- **Develop a perspective for your fears**

One of the ways you can overcome your fear is to sit down and get a real perspective of them. If you are afraid of losing your partner and so you put up with everything they present, then ask yourself if you really have to fear that? What will happen if you actually lose your partner? Will you die? Ask yourself if you would really lose your partner when you set boundaries? What would be the worst thing that could happen because you chose to say no? Will your life end? Will you remain single for the rest of your life? Does a lack of boundaries make you vulnerable to abuse in your relationship? Asking yourself these questions would help you understand if your fears are really even worth fearing in the first place.

- **Make a decision**

Once you have gotten a perspective of your fears, the next thing to do is to make the decision that you are going to overcome them. Put it in your mind that henceforth, you will not let your fears prevent you from making decisions that are beneficial to your life. Have the willpower and determination to overcome those fears come what may. Deciding to get rid of your fears is a step in helping you actually overcome them. Make the decision that you have already absorbed enough in the relationship, and you have decided to set boundaries and leave some room for yourself.

- **Think of the benefits**

Remind yourself of the trouble and problems you have experienced because of your fears. Remember the humiliation and abuse you have been going through and all the benefits that await you once you overcome your fears and set boundaries in your life. Think of the freedom, the fulfillment, the happiness that will come with the ability to say no and put limits to the things that you can take. Reminding yourself of the benefits will help keep you determined to overcome your fears.

- **Evaluate risks**

To overcome your fear of setting boundaries, you have

to sit down and evaluate the risks associated with it. List all the things you think will happen and assess them one after the other. Doing that will help you see clearly the weight of what you fear. You may even be surprised to find out that the risks are not even worth it and that most of what you fear is just in your head.

- **Believe you have the strength**

No matter how scared you are of the consequences of setting boundaries in your life, you need to tell yourself that you can do it. You have the strength required to make those fears part of a memory. Do not let hesitation prevent you from doing something you can do. Do not assume that it is something too tedious, or too demanding for you to be able to do. You have the strength; you have the zeal and all it takes.

- **Start now**

It is high time you stopped fixing dates and making resolutions for when you will set boundaries and take action now. If you keep saying "I will do it today," "I will speak to James tomorrow," "I will leave this till next week," then you may actually never do it. No one is created with a time to do something, and unless you fix your boundaries now, the right time will never come.

•   Seek professional help

If you feel that getting rid of your fears and setting boundaries is not something you can handle on your own, then you should seek help from a professional. You can engage a therapist who will hold your hand and guide you through. It will also help you feel that you are not alone and that someone is there with you. A therapist will also help monitor your progress and keep you in line when you feel like you cannot do it anymore.

Redrawing Boundaries

Once you are set on overcoming your fears and building healthy boundaries, you are already on the road to overcoming codependency. All you need to do is to identify the boundaries you need to set and how to set them. Understand what you like and what you do not like, so that when you talk with your partner, you will be able to make them understand the reason for your actions. There are things you need to remember when trying to set boundaries in order to avoid doing the opposite of what you intend to achieve.

Do not set boundaries while you are angry. Anger can make you emotional and cloud your judgment. Setting boundaries while you are angry may make you set boundaries that are too rigid and which you may later come to dislike. It may also make you attack your partner personally, which is not going to help in making your partner understand. Anger may be the driving force to your setting boundaries, but do not be resentful, and do not set them until it subsides and you become clear-headed enough to do so. Listen closely to yourself and know what you really want. Set boundaries that will meet your immediate needs while at the same time considering those of your partner.

Communicate your new boundaries in clear and easy-to-understand language. Do not use ambiguous words that leave grey areas. Make sure you state what you want clearly so that your partner will not find an excuse by saying they did not get what you actually meant. Put on an expression that says you are serious and really mean what you are saying. Do not set boundaries while you are laughing at it; your partner may think it is a joke. You also shouldn't put on an angry or enraged face that may even make the discussion impossible. Remember also not to talk with a hint of guilt or the feeling that you are doing it in spite of yourself. Make your partner understand that this is something you are doing because you have realized that it is the best thing for you to do. It is not because you are forcing yourself, but because you need to do something for your own sake too.

You have to understand that, at the onset, your partner may not like your new move, your new understanding and sense of self may make him/her feel intimidated. So, **you should not relent**, be steadfast, and maintain your grounds. Make your partner realize the reasons why you cannot continue on the current track. Show them how the state of your relationship is affecting you, and why you need a change of the status you are in. Eventually, your partner may come to understand why you did what you did. And if they don't, what use is a partner that never considers your needs anyway?

Prepare yourself for the worst that may happen. Sometimes, you may have to give an ultimatum or make it clear to your partner what the consequences of not respecting your boundaries will mean. If your partner refuses to consider your own needs and work within the limits of your boundaries, then you may have to bring **an end to the relationship**. No matter what happens, be prepared to take the outcome of your actions, and not feel regretful about it. Assure yourself that if your partner couldn't handle your boundaries, because they would rather enable your codependency, then someone out there will certainly be able to.

In a nutshell, know that the boundaries you set are there to help you grow, take you out of the depression and frustration you have been dealing with because of how much your needs have been ignored; and make you more self-reliant and confident.

You are not setting them because you want to be rude, or distance yourself from others; you are doing it to maintain your identity and have your own needs catered for in all of your relationships. It also doesn't mean that you are going to stop considering other people's or your partners' needs in your relationships. It is a way of finding a balance between you and your partner, without any of you trampling upon the needs or rights of the other.

Healthy borders will boost your confidence and make you happier in your relationships. You will be able to appreciate your partner more if you do not feel that he/she is using you or ignoring your rights. When you see that your partner is considering your own needs and respecting your boundaries, you will love him/her more, and that will make the relationship better and more fulfilling.

WHY THERAPY IS THE KEY TO ACHIEVING THE CONTROL AND SELF-ESTEEM YOU'VE BEEN NEEDING

First Time in Therapy?

The first time I attended a therapy session for my codependency, I went in with lots of ideas about what therapy would be like. Of all the ideas and expectations that went into that neatly arranged office with me, though, the most important and dominant was the fear of opening myself up before a total stranger. If you are seeking therapy as a codependent individual or an empath, your expectations won't be very different from mine.

Society raises us to be conscious of our nudity – it is part of our dignity as humans. But there is another type of nudity that we are very conscious of, that we badly want to protect – the nudity of our mind. One of the greatest achievements of nature is shielding our thoughts from the awareness of others. Life would be chaos if others could hear your thoughts as they hear your words. The closest people can get to knowing what goes on in your mind is to analyze your actions, to read clues on your face and in your speech, or to listen to you spill out your guts. Yet, many problems such as codependency and excessive empathy require that we speak up and be heard, to hear ourselves.

However, not many possess the ability to listen to and understand others, and this is why our closest friends may not be able to help us out. Luckily therapists – trained to figure out what is mentally or emotionally wrong with us – close this gap for us. Whatever name you want to call them, their roses always smell as sweet. Everyone knows that therapists are able to understand and help us by having conversations with us. So, when people are going into therapy for the first time, the fear is about sitting in front of someone who can see through you and help you effect life-saving changes. This notion is as false as it is correct.

The notion is correct because the moment you go into therapy, you become your own autobiography opened wide before the therapist to study. She can flip backward and forward, logically tying together events narrated in this book, notwithstanding that they are separated in both space and time. She may be able to find out that the seeds of your codependency were planted many years ago when you were still the young girl trying to win the approval of your alcoholic dad.

The notion is wrong because therapy is no magic, and therapists are no sorcerers who can pull out your soul from your body. They are humans who can be wrong or right, just as you can. Therapy, therefore, can be equally productive and unproductive, depending on several factors.

Like you probably will, I went into my first session thinking I was going to someone who would see it all. Yes, she saw a lot but not all. I realized I needed to participate, to be willing to receive help and make conscious efforts towards it. I realized I needed to play my part, to be at ease, to open up to my therapist. Only then was my therapist able to engage me meaningfully. Do not go into therapy, thinking it would open you up to a total stranger. Instead, go into therapy, thinking it is opening you up to someone who can teach you how to help yourself.

Another thing you need to realize about your first therapy is that it is usually an introduction to your new relationship. Yes, when you are in therapy, you are in a relationship with your therapist. And no, I am not speaking of her duty of confidentiality to you or the professional relationship she has with you. I am speaking of a relationship of trust; it takes a lot to let go of the reluctance against spilling out your gut to someone you did not know before. So, your first therapy session is usually to prepare the two of you for sessions to come.

Nevertheless, your first session can go deeper than just an introduction. You could dive into the main thing. Your therapist won't be expecting you to want to go deep, but like many persons going into therapy for the first time, you could find yourself too eager to share, to pour out *everything* and expect the therapist to piece it all together. So, in such circumstances, your first session can be like your fifth or sixth when you are already familiar with your therapist and it's now convenient to share with her.

The Scope of Therapy Sessions

When in therapy, we often think our sole role is to answer questions. We think all we have to do is respond to the prompts of the therapist, to speak, listen, and accept what they say about us or our state of mind as the unquestionable truth. But this is wrong. Whether you are in your first session or the tenth one, you must know therapy is not one-way traffic. Some things go both ways, and asking questions is one of them. Do not be the guy that will accept everything he is told hook, line, and sinker. Be the one that will ask questions and seek clarifications when his therapist is not making sense to him.

If you can ask questions during therapy, don't you also

think you can equally disagree? Yes, you can. You can disagree with your therapist. This is what many who go into therapy for the first time do not know, but now you do. And it is important that you know this because your first session can go beyond its usual introductory nature. Why is it important to disagree? A therapist helps you understand yourself by tapping into their own knowledge of human nature and experience in practice. They guide you towards a solution to your problem. But they are humans who can be wrong in their conclusions about you. Only challenging their assessment can help both you and the therapist find the right answers.

Therapy opens your eyes to a whole new book of details about yourself. It reveals the good, the bad, and the ugly in you. You knew all three existed within you, and that's why you went into therapy in the first place. But you are not going into therapy in order to judge yourself, to depress yourself with your guilt. Truly, your misery might have escalated because you refused to seek help in good time. Truly, you might feel guilty for having let your partner sink deeper into the abyss of alcohol addiction by seeking to please him all the time. But you are not going into therapy to feel guilty about opening yourself up. You are going into therapy to find a much clearer perspective of what is going on with you, to admit your fault where necessary, and to find an answer in the end.

Vivian, my therapist, was kind to have extended an invitation to me that very first night. Later, she told me she had to do it because I sounded like I was nearing a tipping point. So, I thought she was going to *cuddle* me, to pamper me and not tell me the whole truth about myself. I was expecting her to be economical with words, with serving me the facts. But I was wrong. I was not in therapy to be cuddled. Cuddling prevents the achievement of the goals of therapy. It serves you half-truths about yourself and your therapist's assessment of your person. Therapy, therefore, cherishes frankness. Your therapists won't shy away from presenting the truth, the whole truth, and nothing but the truth to you at all times. A half-truth is as good as a lie and lying was what you had been doing to yourself before coming to therapy. Therapy, therefore, won't continue the façade.

Therapy can be safe or exhausting. What do I mean by

this? Earlier, I mentioned that you are not in therapy to be judged. This is true despite the fact that you will be telling a total stranger everything you probably have kept a secret for a long time. What you say in therapy can range from the adorable to the despicable. Yet, you will not be judged for it. This is the safety of therapy – it puts you at ease so that you can only wonder later how your therapist had got you to spill out your guts to him/her.

It is exhausting because you may find yourself making very little progress during a session. This happens where you need to deal with certain things, to have some issues resolved before you can move to other things. In situations like this, the repetitive nature of the questions being asked can be annoying. I remember Vivian trying to get me to tell her about my relationship with my dad. Throughout my adult life, that topic was never on the table for discussion. She did some explanations that convinced me I had to tell her about the early years of my life when I had to process many negative feelings related to my father's alcoholism.

Because therapy forces you to bare your soul; because

therapists help you realize, on your own, the nature and impact of your actions; you may cry during a session. Remember, you are not going into therapy to be cuddled; you are in therapy to seek answers, and that starts with admitting certain realities about yourself. Crying in therapy is not necessarily a sign that you have done something evil – it is an indication that there is still a human within you, one that can feel compassion, not only for others but also for himself.

Many people go in for their first session thinking they will come out with their problem solved. As I have explained earlier, this is normal – we find out something is wrong and we quickly want a fix. However, mending humans is never that easy. Even physical wounds take time to heal, and so do psychological ones. The desire for a quick fix is why the first session, which is supposed to be an introduction, can become like subsequent sessions. You must, however, remember that the cure is never immediate – the diamond had to burn under intense heat before it became precious.

I also found out that I felt worse after some sessions. On one of my sessions, I had had to admit to putting my ex-husband's interest over mine because I lacked self-confidence and self-care. The more I resisted; the smarter Vivian had become in helping me realize that. By the time the session ended, I felt worse about myself, and I told her this. She explained that what I felt was normal, that it was me simmering in one of my many realities, and that I would feel better much later once I realize the admission is the beginning of my effort to practice self-care.

Self-therapy

As a codependent or an empath, you may not need to see a therapist in order to help yourself. Alternatively, self-therapy can also be an added help for your therapy sessions. We are now in the world of do-it-yourself and self-help, and a little effort from you can save you a few hundreds or even thousands of dollars in therapy. How? Self-therapy is the solution.

Earlier in this book, I have discussed a number of useful techniques that you can use in the process of self-healing. For example, I have mentioned mindfulness as a tool that can help you come to the realization that there is a problem with you and how you pay attention to your own emotional needs. I have also taught you how to set boundaries as an empath or how to do just that for the purpose of coming face to face with your fears. All of these are proven techniques that I have shared with others, and for this, I have received only positive feedback and gift cards.

Group Therapy and Support Groups

Much like the twelve-step Alcoholic Anonymous program, Co-Dependents Anonymous (CoDA) exists to help codependent individuals to get over their problems with the aid of support from their peers. Support groups typically offer anonymity while allowing you to tap into the large pool of experiences and insight that each meeting represents. It would be very helpful if you can start to attend already.

How Deep?

How deep have you sunk as a codependent or an empath? This sounds counter-intuitive. But you should remember that without suspecting or realizing something is wrong with you, you won't make an attempt to seek help in the first place. One of the goals of this book is to help you realize that you might be a codependent or an empath, and to help you assess how deep your problem is.

Symptoms have been discussed in this book, and I have stressed the fact that it is not until you exhibit all the symptoms that you become a codependent or an empath. A single symptom might even be enough to help you conclude you have a problem. But who says there cannot be more? The truth is that these symptoms are related to one another and the existence of one presupposes that of others. Assessing how many symptoms you exhibit will, therefore, help you decide how deep your problem is.

Have You Failed to Recover?

Supposing you have come to terms with being a codependent or an empath, have you tried using the techniques in this book to help yourself? To put the matter simply, self-help of any kind is like taking aspirin to relieve pain. If the pain persists after some days, you know it's time you saw a doctor. Therefore, it is not all the time you immediately see a therapist about your problem. In fact, trying first to help yourself is a good sign of commitment to healing. However, if after religiously carrying out the lessons you have learned so far, you still don't feel a change, it's about time you saw a therapist.

In this chapter, you have been disabused of the many false notions that accompany people going into therapy for the first time. Most especially, you know therapy is a process that requires time to produce its effects. You also know therapy is not to cuddle you — it employs frankness to help you see the truth about yourself and take actions. But you also know it is not all the time you run off to a therapist. A little commitment to yourself will not only save you a few dollars but also reinforce the whole message in this book — that you can put yourself first and still remain a good person.

YOUR SECRET GIFT THAT ONLY YOU CAN GIVE

The average empath or codependent individual out there on the streets does not know the correct word to describe his personality type. Even when he is able to put a name to the rare gift he has been given; he does not think of it as a privilege. Unfortunately, things are not helped by contemporary literature that seeks to demonize codependents especially. Most of the works on codependents subconsciously put the blame on codependents for being weak or careless about their feelings. Most books put the fault down to a negative tweak of human nature or a warped mentality. That gets most codependent individuals and empaths on the defensive while seeking to regain control over their thoughts and relationships.

If you are going to pick just a single lesson or message

from this book, let it be from these next few paragraphs.

You are not weak! You are not careless! You are not bad!

Being codependent is not an indictment of your weakness. It is not to say you are inferior to others. Living life as an empath does not make you bad. Rather, it is the opposite that stands true.

You are too good for your own good!

Unlike negative traits like narcissism that stem from unpalatable ideals such as selfishness, greed, and psychological insufficiency, you are not a codependent or empath to massage your own ego or cause damage to other people. Rather, it is because you care for others so much that you forget how to care for you first. Instead of viewing yourself as damaged goods, think of yourself instead as someone with raw talent that has not mastered this talent.

Rather than think of codependency or empathy as illnesses that confirm that you have severe problems, think of yourself as a savior armed with the tools to help others. This is because when it boils down to it, every empath and codependent individual is a potential hero who has not mastered his superpowers. The ability to genuinely care for others is a lost trait. Only very few people can care for others, including strangers, without any underlying intentions. If you have been chosen to be an empath or codependent, then you have the "care and love chromosome" imprinted boldly on your mind. You are a superhero who has not mastered his superpowers. You have an unbelievably strong energy field which you have not learned to control, and which is starting to eat you up from the inside.

That is not a disease of your own fault. Far from it! Instead, it is an indictment of human nature's inability to filter some super-emotions not present in the average individual. In much the same way Harry Potter's first spells did not teach me to destroy Horcruxes, you just need to work on your superpower. In pretty much the same way Sherlock Holmes did not learn to tell a story from a footprint in a day, you just need to practice to gain control over your superpower and turn it into positive use.

From where you are sitting right now, it may seem impossible to spot the positive potentials that empathy and codependency possess. I understand and respect why that may appear so. Therefore, let us launch into specific details of your powers, their inestimable benefits, and how to harness them to serve a better, more fruitful purpose. Are you ready?

Empathy as a superpower

I opened my discussion about empathy in Chapter Three with an analogy about having a super-television able to pick up all channels without any subscription or stress. However, this television has no dial or controller to sort out the pictures it receives, rendering it a piece of junk. It represented the mind of an empath with all the accompanying baggage that it can encompass.

Now, imagine that you find a way to actually control this television, and you can begin to view each channel separately and clearly. How awesome would that be? Luckily, as we have explained in the preceding chapters, this is no big-deal for you an empath. You can actually control your energy levels and restrain your tendency to dissolve in other people's pain.

Understand that you have high-energy and frequency levels that you can use to pull up the people you meet daily. Here are a few other potential benefits of being an empath.

• **Spot potentials**

An empath sees way beyond just pain and suffering. You can also tap into positive feeds and tune into people feeling good. Even more important, you do not just discern other people's moods; you can also spot the potential they hold. You are going to come in contact with many people daily, a lot of whom may likely have confidence issues. A lot of the people you are going to interact with have suppressed their own potentials or allowed circumstances to override their desires. Luckily for them, your radar can detect even the subtlest energy flow in the people you meet. You only need to watch people complete a task or speak about their work to know if they really have a passion or potential for that work. That allows you to be an unbeatable source of motivation that they need to establish self-trust and belief. In the same way, you have the ability to analyze situations better and look at the positive sides of even disasters for better and proper management.

- **Become a conduit for positive energy flow by becoming mindful**

An aware empath is the best type of friend anybody can have. Why do I say this? An empath who has developed his gifts is no longer just a bundle of energy and high-frequency flesh and bone. He can actually turn himself into a conduit to spread positive cheer around.

As an empath, you can not only receive energy; you can dispense a whole lot of it as well. Instead of going through life, unaware yourself, adopt mindfulness, and you will be surprised at how effectively you can use that to better the lives of everyone around you. You may come across narcissists who are wired to barge into your frequency and knock you off your stride. But by remaining mindful, and refusing to be drawn into their cesspit, you may even succeed in pulling them out.

- **Enjoy life in a way few people can**

The height of enjoyment is in being sensitive and aware enough to live in each and every moment. What does this mean for people who can key into each moment, such as empaths? They may bear a load of pain bigger than their share, but the converse is also true. They enjoy each moment more than you can ever imagine. If you are an empath, you probably know this already.

An empath can see and feel emotions even from inanimate bodies. A poet may talk about the blossoming of a rose flower or the cascade of a waterfall, but for an empath, these are really more than others can imagine. An empath in a garden actually feels like a part of nature. The threshold for the appreciation of life's finer things is infinitely sharper with empaths. As an empath, you do not just exist within a moment; you have the potential to enjoy and live each moment in such a luxuriant way that no other category of people can.

- **Use body language and eye contact to raise moods**

A smile will always raise the moods of the people we meet each day. A smile is always worth its own weight any day, but it is twice its weight in gold when it comes from a true empath. Why is this so?

An empath is not just going through the motions when he smiles. He actually wants to smile and communicate a mood-changing gesture. Now, not everyone is an empath, but everyone can detect on a subconscious level when a smile is genuine. Therefore, you have the power to lift moods with just the right body language.

The same thing applies to eye contact. The face is the most expressive part of our anatomy, and the eyes are its most expressive part. Eye and facial gestures reach deeper when they are given out by an empath. You have the ability to warm hearts. Use it!

- **Use your vision to lead others**

As an empath, you are able to see through and understand the people around you better than usual. If that is not a foremost leadership quality, then nothing is. Being able to understand the people you want to lead means you will be able to anticipate their needs and disposition, to create enabling leadership for them.

- **Intuition and gut instinct on a superhuman level**

As Colette Davenport opined, "Everybody has intuition, but the gut feelings of empaths are quite literal." We all have intuition; it is our mind's alarm system trying to warn us of impending events that our five sensory organs do not pick up. Sometimes, previous experiences and archived information serve as the basis for these warnings. The most important thing to note is that with empaths, intuition becomes almost the sixth sense, feeding you quality, dependable ideas, and insight on an above-human level. This has many numerous practical applications. For instance, growing up, I could tell to a very high degree of accuracy which of my father's new friends my mother would like. It took me just a few sentences and glances to file most new people I met then into "likable" and not likable."

Codependency as a superpower

If there's one thing codependents are guilty of in a world rife with selfishness, it is too much selfless care and concern that goes too far, for too long. No one can become codependent without possessing high levels of sympathy, tolerance, and concern for their dependent partner. Negative as codependency may be, it does have certain benefits and advantages that make it an almost desirable trait. Taken care of properly, you can tap the origins of codependency to enjoy a better life and impact positively on the people around you. Codependency does not mean that you are too weak. Rather, it says you need to construct clear boundaries that allow you to show care and concern safely without getting consumed in the process of helping others.

- **Genuine compassion and care**

The greatest superpower that you have as a codependent is genuine compassion and care. Very few people are able to actually show compassion in sufficient quantities to the people around them in need of it. Most of the time, the offers of help we get are half-hearted and do not go beyond the surface. A codependent has no such issues though; he is willing to go extra lengths to help at all times. In fact, it is highly important for you to watch the amount of mental energy you commit to helping others as care and concern are wired deeply into your nature.

• Codependents make the greatest friends

One of the primary roles of friendships is to provide us with support in our goals and daily lives. A codependent represents the best bet of deriving that from a friend. It is not entirely healthy for you to be codependent, but on the flip side, it makes you a dependable and reliable friend for all your friends and even family members.

• A genuine nose for uncomfortable scenarios even when you are not an empath

Not all codependents are empaths, but given the extra mental energy that codependents commit to relationships and emotional status, they are more aware than the average guy and lady on the street. In fact, troubleshooting can become too much of an obsession if care is not taken. However, your increased sensitivity also sharpens your radar for detecting potential problems early enough.

• The ability to heal partners

By way of initial intention, codependents want to help

partners and family members so badly that they lose themselves in the process of helping others. Childhood events and psychological imbalances make it possible for the compassion you are trying to show to become pathological sources of emotional instability, but that does not really change the fact that you want your partner to be well. I know it sounds markedly different from what we have said about codependency, but you do not really have a genuine interest to see people suffer. Unfortunately, you are just a victim too, and your initial intention gets lost. If you ever turn the corner though, it is almost impossible for your partners not to improve and deal with their addictions. The intention to heal and the ability to feel concerned can help launch your partner into an unstoppable drive to get rid of their addictions.

To close this chapter, let me hit you with the key points again. Codependency and empathy do not make you a bad person. In fact, most of the time, they developed outside your control. However, they are a part of you and manifest in the bulk of your emotional decisions. There is no need for you to feel ashamed of them. In fact, they also have benefits that you can enjoy as you make the journey to limit their impacts on your life.

Like every other superpower, you need to practice and get control over empathy and your tendency to be codependent. Using the positives that abound, you can make yourself a beacon of fresh, mental energy that cares for you and those around you within healthy margins that do not overwhelm you.

CONCLUSION

Relationships are a vital part of our existence as humans; they are meant to protect and help us enjoy more from life by working in tandem with the people around us that we count as friends, partners, and family members. Unfortunately, relationships do not always end up as being beneficial or very helpful, especially when the other party is a self-immersed narcissist. It is these sorts of situations that give rise to codependency and the makings of an empath.

To be frank, being an empath with no active filter to screen you from the emotions of other people causes a mental overload where you lose sight and control of the bigger pictures. Every negative signal from everyone around triggers negative reactions in you that you do not seem to be able to control. This means your mood is going to be affected by extraneous circumstances outside your control or responsibility. In fact, you lose all semblance of control over your mood and certain decisions. That leaves you susceptible to a million other problems.

Codependency, on the other hand, develops from being so good and caring to others that you become addicted to being caring. That exhausts you and leaves you hankering after praise. If you are unfortunate enough to live or care for a narcissist or a manipulator, things become even worse as you are playing a losing game.

Codependency and empathy, therefore, develop from essentially positive and good intentions, which we lose control of. Forget the underlying causes though; they are bad for you if you do not take back control of your thought process and reward system. They will run your emotional and mental batteries into the ground if you leave them unchecked. They will leave you sore, grossly deficient and mentally insufficient. That is why you must take action, seek therapy today, and get on the recovery road.

You cannot fix other people if you are broken yourself, and that is exactly what you are going to be if you keep on fixing others without recourse to your own emotional and mental needs. It is not selfishness to put yourself first. You are not self-centered if you do not allow others to manipulate you into damaging your mental health for their own sakes. Yes, it is your responsibility to feel empathy for others, and cater for loved ones, but that does not give you the exclusive position of "chief caregiver." You cannot give what you do not have in reserve, and if you keep giving without recharging, you will end with nothing in your reserve tank.

Therefore, you **must** seek therapy to deal with the dangers of unhealthy and toxic relationships. As an empath, you must learn to scale your energy up and deflect all attempts to bring you down into a receptive mode. Allow the words of Andrew Boyd to inspire your journey to higher mental realms. He said,

"When you feel connected to everything, you also feel responsible for everything. And you cannot turn away. Your destiny is bound with the destinies of others. You must either learn to carry the Universe or be crushed by it. You must grow strong enough to love the world, yet empty enough to sit down at the same table with its worst horrors."

As a codependent, you have to relearn the concepts of care and concern. You cannot offer yourself up each time a sacrifice is required. You cannot continue to live your life from within thy eyes of a loved one or loved ones. Nobody is more important than you. Nobody's problems supersede yours in importance even if they are more urgent. By all means, inconvenience yourself from time to time to help other people. It is a basic requirement of being human. However, learn to delineate and define your outer limits. You do not even help others when you take so much care of them that they can no longer stand on their own feet. As Erol Ozan said, "Help someone, you earn a friend. Help someone too much; you make an enemy."

Do not be the candle that extinguishes itself to give light to others. Do not allow your "hero" chromosome deceive you into *killing* yourself for others to live. You will not even be missed for the right reasons if you care so much that you disappear into a mental whirlpool. Life will go on as always.

Understand that as a codependent and/or an empath, you have unique characteristics that make it impossible for you not to seek greater emotional control, if you must enjoy the healthy fruits of the relationships you are in.

Being an empath is a rare gift; one that you must harness and learn to use safely. If you do not, you will get crushed by the universe and the people within it. Being codependent is a rare trait that gives you boundless amounts of compassion and care to give away. If you do not learn to control the compulsion to help others at all costs, you will eventually give yourself away too.

Learn to see without getting blinded!

Begin to feel without being pulled in!

Understand that you need to care without going overboard!

Love but do not exist to only help!

Above all, love yourself above any other thing. Understand that you are a separate entity responsible for his own emotional security first before any other thing. Do not get deceived into giving up your own life to live the life of other people. You are responsible for you first and foremost. Be aware and take care of yourself first. In fact, cater to your own mental and emotional needs at all times. **If you do not, why should anybody else?**

Good Luck!

RESOURCES

- Beattie, Melody. *(1992).* Codependent no more : how to stop controlling others and start caring for yourself. [Center City, MN] :Hazelden,

- CoDA, (1997). *Co-Dependents Anonymous*, CoDA Resource Publishing, Phoenix,

- Knudson, M.T., and Terrell, H.K. (2012). Codependency, Perceived Interparental Conflict, and Substance Abuse in the Family of Origin. *American Journal of Family Therapy,* 40(3):245-257 Retrieved August 22, 2019, from https://www.researchgate.net/publication/2417 18531_Codependency_Perceived_Interparental _Conflict_and_Substance_Abuse_in_the_Famil y_of_Origin

- Lancer, Darlene. (2012). Codependency for dummies. Hoboken, NJ : John Wiley & Sons

- Lancer, Darlene. (2014). *Conquering Shame and Codependency: 8 Steps to Freeing the True You*, Hazelden, Minnesota,

- Springer, C. A., Britt, T. W., & Schlenker, B. R. (1998). Codependency: Clarifying the construct. *Journal of Mental Health Counseling, 20*(2), 141-158.

CPSIA information can be obtained
at www.ICGtesting.com
Printed in the USA
LVHW090334030420
652108LV00005B/1393